Legal War Stories: A Memoir

John Gould

Legal War Stories: A Memoir

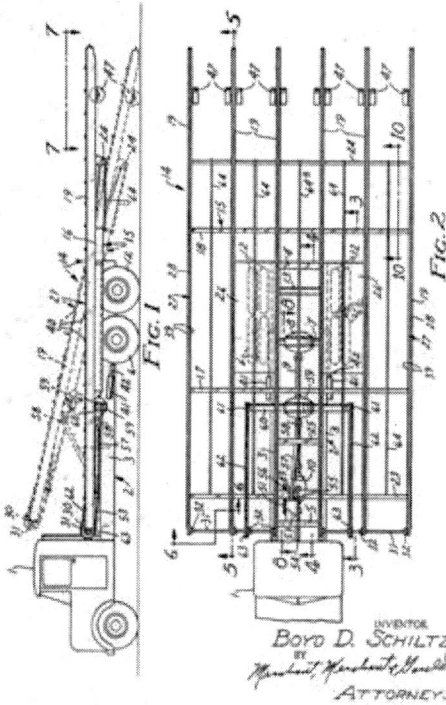

By

John Gould

DEDICATION

This book is dedicated to all the great lawyers I have had the privilege of working with at Merchant & Gould. Some are deceased, some are fully retired, some went to work with clients, some went on to start their own firms and some are still at Merchant & Gould.

PREFACE

A. Letter

As very busy lawyers, we sometimes don't have time left in the day for our families. I know I was away from home a lot, at trial, traveling to take depositions, at hearings, etc. One of my sons recently sent me a copy of a letter I wrote to my children some forty-one years ago. As I read it, it seemed good enough to include here:

November 22, 1969
A Letter to My Children

I have never been much of a letter writer. I was quite prolific for just a brief time when, prior to our marriage, your mother worked in New York, and I was in Minneapolis. However, now that I have recently embarked upon "serious" letter writing (i.e., to the president, etc)., perhaps a letter to you may be a way to say a few things that lie in the heart but are sometimes difficult to communicate. If you wish to "write" me, you know that I would like to hear from you.

Where does one begin? Perhaps at the beginning; although it should be obvious, even this sometimes needs to be expressed. Each one of you means very much to your mother and me. We are concerned with you about your hopes, your dreams, your problems, your life today, your growth to maturity, your happiness.

One thought for you to tuck away for future use, if necessary: you must always remember that no matter what may come to you in life, we love you. This transcends all other factors in our relationships with you. Yes, we may have certain hopes and concerns for you, and we may be right or we may be wrong in some of the things we do for you, with you, or, as you may feel, against you, but whatever we do is because of love. After you leave home, we cannot and should not (and don't want to) "direct" your affairs. If it is any comfort, at any time, feel secure that our concern and love will not diminish.

What does a father hope or want for his children? To be famous? To be wealthy? To be powerful? No.

I hope that my children will be healthy.

Healthy in mind.

Each of you are intelligent, which I hope you will use to the fullest, but this means more than intelligence. To me, it means that one is able to meet all of the various feelings and attitudes of life successfully. Each person, at sometime or another in his life, shall know both sorrow and joy. Be able to meet and overcome sorrow, discouragement, failure, ridicule, and sickness, and be able to accept, enjoy, and share your joys, successes, praise, and friendships. If you are discouraged, do not give up. If you are successful, have joy in it, but do not let it go to your head. Your life should involve more than personal success. If you think one is born with a healthy mind and that is the end of it, one way or the other, and that it never changes and does not require any work or effort on your part, I feel that you may be wrong. It is a challenge and it does require work and effort to "try to know one's self." I believe that one's attitude towards himself, others, and his work are important. I believe it to be important not to destroy one's mind with self-pity, selfishness, hatred, fear, envy, greed, and drugs or pep pills.

Healthy in body.

You are all healthy in body now, and I hope you will stay that way. Why? Because you will be happier if you do. Of course, this will also require some work and effort on your part. There are many hazards running the gamut from drugs to careless use of an automobile, from mere lack of exercise to gluttony. On lack of exercise, I could practice some of my own preaching.

I hope my children will be self-confident most of the time. I say most of the time because, like many things, our ego has its ups and downs. And by self-confidence, I mean confidence in your ability to live. Do not be afraid of life. All people are born, and all people will die. In between is all the life on this earth that we have. Make good use of your time for now and for the future. An arrogant person is not a self-confident person. A bully or cruel person cannot be self-confident. It is not necessary to feel that one is "best" to be self-confident. Each of you has the ability to live useful lives. Be confident in that ability.

I hope that my children are honest with themselves and with others. Why? Life can be hard at times under the best of circumstances. But if one becomes filled with deceit and distrust, life can be nothing but trouble and unhappiness. Remember also that "trust" is sometimes so difficult to build and yet so easily broken.

I hope that my children will be willing to work. I have a theory that a person is happier if they are working. What the work is, is not so important. But it should be "work," a challenge for the mind, body, or heart and not merely something to fill the hours between breakfast and dinner.

I hope my children will look beyond self-interest to the interests of others. I don't mean to be religious in this letter, but the following Commandments are worth trying to be made a part of one's life:

The First Commandment is that thou shalt love the Lord thy God with all thy heart, soul, and mind; and the Second is like unto it, love they neighbor as thyself.

And if you are healthy in body and mind, self-confident, honest, willing to work, and thoughtful of others, I believe you will be happy in your life–no matter where you go or what you do.

All that I want for you is that you find some happiness in your life.

Having touched generally on love and happiness, my next letter will perhaps have to probe more into specific important areas, which will be of help to you during the years ahead. Such as, "How to swim in deep water with your boots on, hands tied behind your back, and blindfolded without a canoe, food, or matches until an optical phenomenon produced by the presence of a stratum of hot air of varying density across which one sees reflections, usually inverted and often distorted, of some distant shore comes into view and from which comes help.

Love,
Dad

B. Introductory Comments

If I do not start, I will never get this project done. I am going to try to write about my trial experiences. War stories, they are called. I will start with the fact that I graduated from Marshall High School, Minneapolis, in early June 1945. For the record, I was valedictorian. I had enlisted in the navy early that year to go with other classmates to Radar School. I believe Stuart Aaker, Tup Way, and Thorson were fellow Radar participants.

At first, because of the end of the war in Europe, they were closing down the school, but we ended up going to classes in Chicago. Then, I was in aviation electronics and assigned to Corpus Christi for further training in repair of aviation radio and radar gear. We were told we had received a five-thousand-dollar education in electrical engineering, so it was natural for me to enroll in the Electrical Engineering program in the College of IT at the University of Minnesota. I was two years in EE when I became disenchanted with it as a career path. (I have always blamed a boring course in winding DC motors as the impetus to change direction.)

I first took the available battery of tests at the U of M to tell me what I should do. They were not much help except to say I would be good at sales, maybe acting. I had two older brothers in law school, and I looked into combining my engineering courses with law. I shifted my major in IT to a BS in physics, where I thought I would receive a broader based technical education. I really enjoyed my chemistry classes and did well in them. I graduated in the spring of 1950 with a bachelor of physics with distinction.

I was very tempted and encouraged at the university to go on in graduate work in chemistry at Stanford, but I got a summer job as a clerk in Honeywell's patent department the summer of 1950. During that summer, I ran into a high school classmate, Mary Ravlin, and we went on a few dates. Mary had just graduated from Smith and was due to start a job in New York City at the public library, living with a couple of girlfriends in her brother Jim's apartment in Stuyvesant Town.

In the fall of 1950, before starting law school, I visited Mary in NYC and became encouraged that we were destined to be married. A courtship by mail ensued. That fall, about Thanksgiving, I bought a ring, we became engaged, and March 27, 1951, we were married. It must have been spring break from law school.

The summer of 1951, I worked again as a clerk in Honeywell's patent department. I was the first summer clerk hired by Honeywell in its legal department. George Fisher was head of the department. Henry Hanson, one of Honeywell's patent lawyers, became a good friend and mentor.

At that time, the patent lawyers had small cubicles that were their offices. They had glass partitions that permitted George to keep track of his minions. My leaving my own cubicle to chat with other lawyers was considered a waste, and I was encouraged not to do it. Fortunately, I was not deterred, and I learned a lot. One thing I learned was that I did not want to work for Honeywell when I graduated.

Meanwhile, I convinced Fisher to let me write a patent application the summer of 1951. I was, of course, supervised by a registered patent lawyer. So, the summer of 1952, I planned to get a job with a patent law firm. I was told that Art Caine, a sole practitioner with the firm of Whitely and Caine, was looking for someone, but I first tried the large firm of Williamson, Schroeder, Adams & Myers. Ev. Schroeder thought they could use someone like me, but fortunately, the boss, George Williamson, did not think so. So, I went to work with Art Caine as a summer clerk, a position that continued through my entire senior year in law school.

I might digress a moment to state that with three years of law school ahead of me, I thought I would get a master's in EE. It turned out that I had taken advanced EE courses in my physics program, but I lacked bachelor credits. I convinced the EE department to let me make up the bachelor EE credits for my master's. I would have to write a thesis. Therefore, during my first year of law school, I was also taking EE courses. After one year of that, I made the brilliant decision that since I was married, was on the Law Review, etc., I didn't need a master's degree.

Art Caine was a wonderful employer for me. He was British-born from the Isle of Man. He was very conscientious and thoroughly supervised my patent application writing. During my senior year of law school, I wrote the briefs on a Seventh Circuit appeal that Art had. I graduated from the University of Minnesota Law School in June of 1953, took the bar exams that summer, and was admitted to practice as a lawyer in September 1953.

In October 1953, Art let me argue that part of the Seventh Circuit Appeal relating to unfair competition. We didn't win, but it was a wonderful experience that young lawyers today would not be able to have. I was with Art as a lawyer for almost a year when I thought I needed a fifty-dollar-a-month raise. Starting salaries were generally $250 a month, but with my prior degree, I believe my starting salary with Art was $275. My request for a fifty-dollar raise was turned down.

I had heard that Merchant & Merchant had been looking for a new hire so I interviewed with Ralph Merchant. He agreed to the fifty-dollar-a-month raise and said that he would try me for six months. I started with Merchant & Merchant on April 1, 1954. The six-month trial period was never discussed. When I wrote my first patent application for the firm, I took it in for Ralph to review as Art had. Ralph took all of thirty seconds to thumb through it, said it was great, and told me to do more like it, and that concluded my training in writing patent applications. Merchant & Merchant consisted of Ralph; his older brother Harvey, who was not a lawyer but a patent attorney (agents admitted to practice before a certain date could call themselves patent attorneys although they were not lawyers); Art Ringsrud, a patent agent; Virginia Brady, receptionist, secretary, and bookkeeper; Dick Lund, draftsman; and two or three secretaries. I was the second lawyer. Our offices were in the Rand Tower.

The first year and a half with Ralph, I wrote a lot of patent applications, about seventy. I have printed out several of those patents, and they are very interesting. Many were for clients who are still with the firm. U.S. patent 2,809,709 was for a muffler or silencer for the Donaldson Company; several patents were for Kermit Wilson of Sico Inc. see U.S. 2,747,958 (which was reissued as 24,454); U.S. 2,800,922 was for Lynn Charlson's hydraulic valve, whose company, the Char-Lynn Company, was the forerunner in manufacturing and selling hydraulic motors for the auto industry; U.S. 2,787,089 was for the Paul E. Hawkinson Company, the pioneer of tire retreading; U.S. 2,848,003 was for a change-making mechanism of A. R. Gross, of Gross-Given Company, a pioneer in vending machines; U.S. 2,756,855 was for an invention of Dale Kloss of Champion Motors Company, one of the early out-board motor manufacturers; U.S. 2,805,839 was for a fluid pressure operated jack of Charles E. Branick of Branick Industries, Fargo, North Dakota.

I mentioned my start in litigation with Art Caine in 1953. When I started with Ralph Merchant, he was very glad to have a young eager lawyer willing to work on litigation.

Contents

MY FIRST TRIAL

My first case with Ralph was a suit filed in New York City, Bechik Products Inc. v. Flexible Products Inc. et al. Bechik Products made mattress accessories, including mattress handles. Ralph had successfully handled a very important interference for Mike Bechik and had also successfully sued Flexible Products for infringement of an earlier Bechik patent. Upon expiration of that patent, Flexible Products was back in business infringing upon an improved mattress handle patent, U.S.RE 22,807.

Upon commencement of the suit, Flexible Products brought a motion to enjoin Bechik Products from representing that defendant corporation or any of its customers were infringing Bechik's patent and from instituting suits against Flexible Product's customers. I went by myself to NYC loaded for bear to argue against this motion. I hardly had time to say anything when the court granted the defendant's motion. This was not a propitious beginning to my career as a litigator.

The firm's good friend, Morris Kirschstein of NYC, handled the appeal of this injunction to the Second Circuit Court of Appeals. The decision, reported at 225 F.2d 603 (2d Cir. 1955), held that the injunction against customers may issue only upon Flexible furnishing a suitable bond. The District Court was reversed and the case remanded for entry of a modified order. Flexible Products failed to enter the bond, and Bechik was free to sue customers of Flexible Products. It did not take us long to commence suit in a jurisdiction other than NYC.

The first suit I tried was Bechik Products Inc. v. New & Frank Co. Inc. in Chicago before Judge La Buy. Ralph went with me for the trial. We put on a wonderful case of commercial success with equipment in the courtroom demonstrating the making of the mattress handle. One of the features of the patent was that it was replaceable. Most important was the use of it in the manufacturing of mattresses. Mike Bechik was on the stand for cross-examination when the defendant's counsel asked the court for a brief recess to bring in a mattress for Mr. Bechik's cross. It struck me (why I hadn't prepared for this, I cannot explain) that the defendant was going to ask Mike Bechik to replace the mattress handle, and I didn't know if he would be able to do it. I immediately asked the court if it would possible to interrupt Mr. Bechik's cross for me to call an out-of-town witness who was expected to testify that day but was prevented by the length of the Bechik cross. This was a true statement to the court. The defendant's counsel not only agreed to the interruption of Bechik's cross, but asked if they could put a witness on out of order. I, of course, agreed, and by the time both witnesses had testified, the day was over. Ralph, Mike Bechik, and I were at a mattress factory in Chicago at 6:00 the next morning doing three things:

1. We had the Chicago company commence making a mattress with softer side walls than current mattresses;

2. We had Mike Bechik practice replacing a handle; and

3. I lined up a very strong worker at the factory, who was not very bright, but he could tie a mattress into a pretzel. If Mike could not replace the handle (because of his age), this witness could.

So, we were all in court the next morning, and—surprise—the defendant's counsel asked Mike Bechik to demonstrate the replaceability of the handle. Without describing it in detail, Mike did so and upon returning to the stand, stated, "Any housewife can do that!"

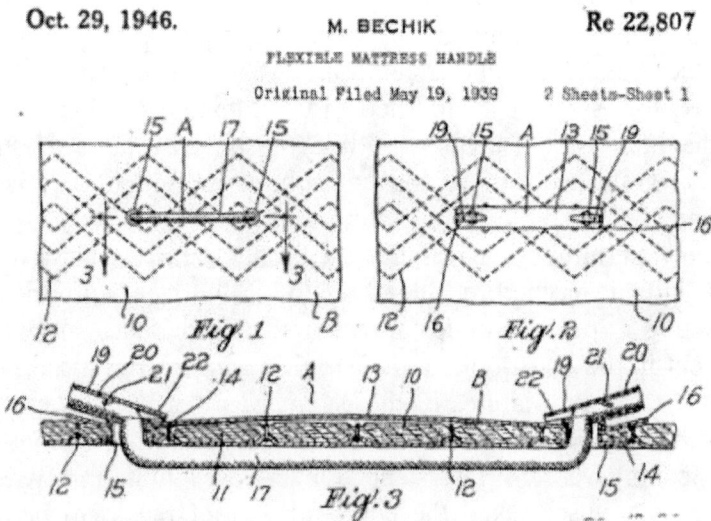

Oct. 29, 1946.   M. BECHIK   Re 22,807

FLEXIBLE MATTRESS HANDLE

Original Filed May 19, 1939   2 Sheets-Sheet 1

Fig. 1   *Fig. 2*   *Fig. 3*

Ralph Merchant cross-examined the defendant's expert witness, but I handled all other aspects of the trial. This was the last case where Ralph appeared in court.

Patent held valid and infringed. *Bechik Products Inc. v. New & Frank Co. Inc.*, 113 USPQ 32 (N.D. Ill 1957).

Moral of this war story: be prepared to rapidly adjust during a trial to unexpected contingencies, but more important, prepare for them before trial.

I have always been very proud of the briefs I wrote and filed in this case. Our main brief was only ten printed pages, and my reply brief was fourteen pages. I still have copies of these briefs.

WACO MFG. CO. V. SYMONS CLAMP MFG. CO

Waco was an acronym for Wilson-Albrecht Company. It was started and owned by Kermit Wilson and Henry (Heinie) Albrecht. They were in the business of making scaffolding, bleachers, concrete wall forms, and other products. Waco was charged with infringing U.S. Patent 2,702,422 and with unfair competition.

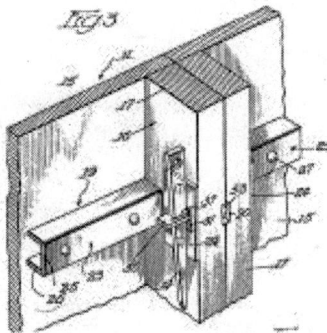

Feb. 22, 1955   A. H. SYMONS   2,702,422
CONCRETE WALL FORM
Filed July 24, 1950   3 Sheets-Sheet 3
Fig. 3

Ralph Merchant must have had some difficulty in persuading Wilson & Albrecht that a twenty-eight-year-old lawyer was competent to handle this important case. Waco filed suit for declaratory judgment that the patent was invalid and that Waco had not committed any acts of unfair competition. Symons Clamp & Mfg. Co., the defendant, promptly filed suit in the N.D. of Illinois against Waco, Henry Albrecht, and two Illinois customers.

I brought a motion in the Minnesota case to enjoin that suit in Chicago pending resolution of the first filed case in Minnesota. Judge Nordbye denied that motion, *Waco Mfg. Co. v. Symons Clamp & Mfg. Co.*, 107 USPQ 115 (D. MN. 1955). Fortunately, we were able to move the Minnesota case along and go to trial before Judge Nordbye.

In discovery, I developed the fact that Symons Clamp had sold a version of their patented clamp more than a year before the patent filing date. This fact invalidated the patent's broadest claims. The defendant disavowed those claims and moved to dismiss them from the case in order to proceed only with the patent's narrower claims, which were different from the product first sold. I opposed this because I wanted to keep those invalid claims in the case. Again, I was unsuccessful.

I seem to have only my reply brief and not a copy of the main brief filed in the case, but this reply points up a strategy I used in the case. I had prepared a large chart showing the defendant's sales before the invention and its sales after the invention. It is a straight line chart showing no spike in sales as a result of the defendant's invention. The defendant had contended that the addition of bearing tongues to its 1950 wall form construction (the prior art on sale, which invalidated the defendant's broad claims) meant the difference between failure and success. As shown by my chart, previously referred to, the defendant's sales in 1950 were approximately $1,323,000, and in 1951, with the addition of the bearing tongues, its sales were $1,635,000. As was argued, the sales prior to 1951 of over $1,000,000 could hardly be contended to be a failure, and if the addition of the tongues had meant the difference between success and failure, this would be indicated by a sudden and sharp vertical rise in a graph of the defendant's volume of business.

This chart was an important and effective trial exhibit. This case also had an important unfair competition claim by Symon's Clamp. I do not have a clear recollection of this trial, but I handled all aspects on my own, including the writing of the briefs.

The case is reported as *Waco Mfg. Co. v. Symons Clamp & Mfg. Co.*, 113 USPQ 270 (D. Mn. 1957). The case was decided by Chief Judge Gunnar Nordbye; counsel for the defendant was Norman Gerlach of Chicago. The companion case in Chicago was dismissed as a result of the decision in this case.

GLENDENNING V. MACK ET AL

This case related to a pants hanger. I represented defendants G. E. Mack Company, marketing the pants hanger, and Fortner & Perrin Inc., the manufacturer of the "Topper" pants hanger. The plaintiff filed suit for infringement of U.S. Patent 2,171,693 on July 8, 1954, so I must have started my litigation career shortly after starting with Ralph Merchant.

The suit was won by the defendants on a decision by Judge Nordbye dated January 22, 1958. The case is reported at 159 F. Supp. 665, 116 USPQ 249 (D. Mn. 1958). I have no recollection of this trial other than the fact that the plaintiff was represented by John Adams of Williamson, Schroeder, Adams & Meyers.

Sept. 5, 1939.   O. D. GLENDENNING   2,171,693

TROUSERS HANGER

Filed June 22, 1938

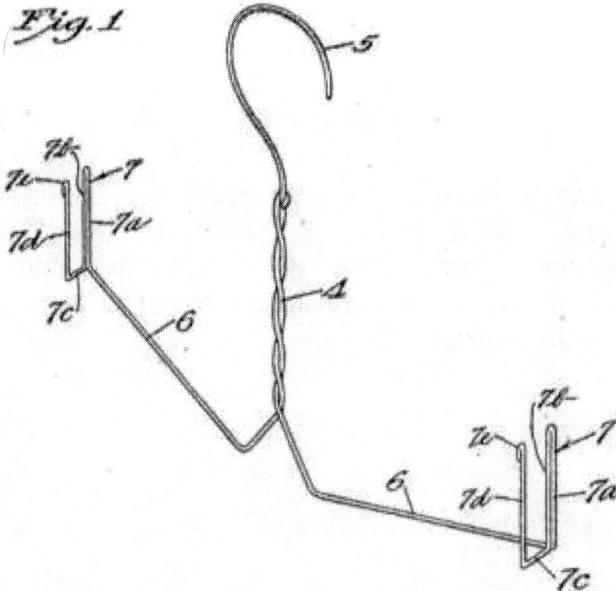

Fig.1

It is now interesting to me that this case, the Bechik case, and the Waco case were all favorably decided within a year—Bechik on March 7,1957, Waco on March 28, 1957, and Glendenning on January 22, 1958. I must have had a very busy time between April 1954 and December 1957, with three lawsuits tried, briefs written, and some seventy patent applications written.

Perhaps it was after I had tried the Glendenning and Waco cases before Judge Nordbye that Mary and I went to a Minnesota State Bar Association dinner. We arrived a little late, and the only seats available were in front at a table of dignitaries, including Judge Nordbye. He introduced me to the others at the table and commented, "John was a very good lawyer for a young man."

SCHAEFER INC. V. MOHAWK CABINET CO.

This case is memorable to me for several reasons. First, Harvey Merchant went with me to Utica, New York, where this case was tried, to help me during the trial. Second, the appeal of this case to the Second Circuit gave me the opportunity to argue before the famous Judge Learned Hand.

Our client, Schaefer Inc., had been charged with infringing Mohawk's patent U.S. 2,750,758 and charged with unfair competition. We filed suit for Schaefer for declaratory judgment of no infringement and no unfair competition in New York, the residence of the defendant, because we deemed it to be a more favorable jurisdiction at that time. I have forgotten the names of the owners of Schaefer, but this was a very important case for them. The outcome would determine whether the company would remain in business. I remember Ralph telling me that Schaefer had given us (me) enough rope to hang ourselves. In other words, spare no expense … but win. The suit was commenced on August 20, 1956, and probably tried in early spring of 1958.

The defendants were represented by Willard Hayes and George Mobille of Cushman, Darby & Cushman of Washington, DC. The judge was a Mr. Brennan. I remember him commenting that they chose the wrong Brennan for the U.S. Supreme Court. The courtroom in Utica was being used for another trial, so we tried this case in the library of the courthouse. It was not a big room, and it made for close intimacy with the judge and the participants.

We must have cited a large number of prior art patents to invalidate the patent in suit. I remember, in opening statements, Willard Hayes commenting on the large number of patents we had to rely on as a reason of no invention. In response, I informed the court that, no, we were relying on a single anticipatory reference. The invention of the patent was an open-top refrigerated display case, alleged to be frost free. The patented cabinet had met with unusual commercial success.

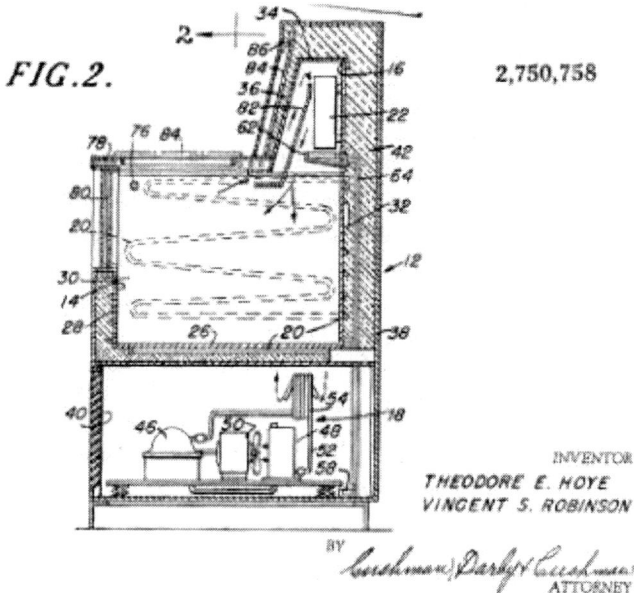

FIG.2.

2,750,758

INVENTOR
THEODORE E. HOYE
VINCENT S. ROBINSON

BY
ATTORNEY

After a day of trial, Harvey and I were walking around the neighborhood, and we saw a delicatessen about a block and a half from the courthouse with a patented cabinet full of frost. I believe our expert had already testified, but we recalled him to testify about this cabinet, serial number, etc., and the amount of frost on its walls. We had no idea how long the cabinet had been in service, whether fans or some other condition had occasioned the frost. We only knew it was a patented cabinet within a short walk from the courthouse, which was not frost free but full of frost. Whether the judge ever viewed this cabinet, we do not know. But he knew where it was.

After we had finished the trial, Judge Brennan commented that he liked to let counsel know his current thinking on the case. He announced he was inclined to hold the patent invalid but that he would like counsel to come back after lunch to present oral argument while the case was fresh in his mind. Willard Hayes told the court that they would prefer to file written briefs. Judge Brennan replied that he wanted counsel to file briefs but also to present oral argument that afternoon.

In spite of the court's wishes for oral argument, Willard Hayes declined the opportunity to do so. I, of course, deferred to his wishes in view of the court's expressed view of the case. Judge Brennan said he could see we all wanted to get home and he wished us Godspeed. Judge Brennan's decision is reported at 165 F. Supp. 688, 118 USPQ 411 (N.D. N.Y. 1958).

The defendant appealed to the Court of Appeals for the Second Circuit. The court sat in Manhattan near Wall St. I was initially pleased with the panel that included one district judge sitting by designation. I thought he might be inclined to uphold his fellow district judge.

Although we were originally scheduled for a morning hearing, we were informed that our hearing was rescheduled for the afternoon because of a change in panel. Learned Hand came in to replace my district judge. Willard Hayes and George Mobille were ecstatic over this change of panel. Our district judge had relied on the U.S. Supreme Court decision of *A&P v. Supermarket Equipment Corp.* Willard Hayes had been counsel in the *Lyon v. Bausch & Lomb* decision by Learned Hand, which had held the 1952 patent act had in effect created a lower standard of invention than required by the A&P case. In argument, George Mobille was pointing out to Judge Hand the prior art patent relied on by us.

Judge Hand was fumbling through the record, trying to find it, and I was gloating over counsel's loss of time for argument. George Mobille did a good job. Judge Hand closed the book, and it was my turn. I had made some comment on infringement, and Judge Hand said, "If I find one claim valid and infringed, that's enough, isn't it?" I replied yes, but that in this case, he could not find one claim valid and infringed. I could see I was getting a very cold stare from the court, and I kept approaching the invalidity issue from different points.

Finally, I saw Judge Hand smile. He turned to the judge on his right and nodded. He turned to the judge on his left and nodded. I had made my point.

Judge Hand, in his decision at 276 F.2d 204, 125 USPQ 318 (2d Cir. 1960), held, "We agree that *Lyon v. Bausch & Lomb Optical Co.* has restored the original test of invention. The precedents which antedate the Bausch & Lomb decision are not necessarily to be disregarded. For example, *Great Atlantic & Pacific Tea Co. v. Supermarket Equipment Corp.*, 340 U.S. 147 (1950), requiring closer scrutiny of combination patents, seems most felicitous here."

Willard Hayes told me later that it was too bad old Judge Hand had become senile to arrive at such a decision. I thought he was still brilliant.

A brief comment: Harvey was very worried about leaving his wife, Winnie, who was diabetic, alone for so long while we were at trial in Utica. Harvey died not too long after this trial from a heart condition. Winnie went on to live by herself for at least thirty more years, playing golf and bowling at ninety years of age.

CHISHOLM RYDER CO. V. T. HOWARD PAULSON AND PAULSON BROTHERS INDUSTRIES INC.

This is a very interesting case for several reasons. First, the Paulson Brothers were eighteen-year-old identical twins, except one was right-handed and the other left-handed. Their father, Howard Paulson of Clayton, Wisconsin, worked for the Stokely Van Camp Company that used equipment purchased from the Chisholm Ryder Company (CRCO) of New York. These were large bean-picking machines integral with a tractor. The Paulson brothers had a concept of building a two-row tractor-pulled bean-picking machine. Howard financed the twins to build two machines, which were leased to the Stokely Van Camp Company. Some people in Texas heard of the machines, and they leased the two machines for use that winter in Texas for $6,000 each.

The Paulsons found themselves in a very profitable business building bean pickers in competition with CRCO. The Paulsons' machine had the advantage over CRCO's machine in being tractor pulled rather than integral with a tractor. If the tractor of CRCO's machine broke down, the bean picker was out of business. With the Paulsons' machine, if the tractor broke down, you merely used a different tractor.

Also, there was a big price difference because you did not have to buy a tractor with the Paulsons' bean picker. So, the Paulsons were sued on January 30, 1959, for infringement of two patents in the Western District of Wisconsin. Leila Ward was the inventor of U.S. Patent 2,587,553, known as the Rake Patent, and John Ward was the inventor of U.S. Patent 2,675,663, known as the moldboard patent. During the winter of 1948–1949, John Ward had built a tractor-mounted, two-row bean picker having two picking reels. This machine included the moldboard and other alleged improvements of the moldboard patent. The machine was successfully tested in Texas(more about this later) in the summer of 1949. It received favorable publicity, and in January 1950, this machine was turned over to CRCO to serve as a model for the bean harvesters built by CRCO. CRCO licensed the patents from the Wards.

John Ward resided in or near Utica, New York. When I had finished the Schaefer case, I felt that if I never returned to Utica, it would be too soon. And, here, my next case, I was returning to Utica, New York, to take the deposition of John Ward. I have no recollection of the inventor Leila Ward; perhaps she was deceased.

The twins had made very large drawings of their machine. They would work at opposite sides of the drawing, one right-handed and one left-handed, and meet in the middle to complete the drawing. The Paulsons were also represented by Warren Knowles of New Richmond, Wisconsin, who later became governor of Wisconsin.

We had a young associate in the office, whose name escapes me. He was supposedly a friend of the judge, and I didn't think it would hurt to have him at counsel table. That was all he was good for. He was never around after a day of trial to help get ready for the next day. He wasn't with us long, and unfortunately, after he was no longer with us, he died climbing the bluff at the St. Croix River.

My patent expert was John Strait, a professor in engineering in the Agricultural School at the University of Minnesota. He was just as straight as his name—a wonderful person and a great expert. This was his first trial as an expert. I was a little worried because my judge was hard of hearing and John was very soft-spoken. We had developed a wonderful piece of prior art: a horse-drawn bean harvester with a picking reel similar to the Rake patent.

Several interesting events at trial.

The twins had insisted they had designed their machine completely independently and without knowledge of CRCO's machine. This may have been true, but the machines were so similar that such testimony was not creditable. I finally convinced the twins that perhaps they had forgotten their father talking about the incredible CRCO machines used to pick beans at Stokely Van Camp. So we were able to develop very creditable testimony on their machine development. Just one problem—have you had an eighteen-year-old witness testify about his machine development? I would ask a question in preparation for trial, and the response was "yeah." No narrative. Warren Knowles was a big help in preparing one of the twins to testify at trial. When on the stand, one of the twins testified how he and his brother had this idea for a tractor-pulled machine, and they wanted to build one to earn money for college. This "story" was too much for CRCO's New York counsel. So, he tried to break down the witness's testimony by asking:

Q. Where are you going to college?

A. Augsburg.

Q. Why are you going there?

A. My mother went there.

I've forgotten how it came about, but the judge got interested in this line of questioning and asked about whether he had paid any tuition yet. The New York lawyer then asked:

Q. Well, just when are you supposed to start college?

A. It depends on how long you keep talking; we were supposed to start yesterday.

No more questions.

Two events occurred during John Strait's cross-examination. First, I mentioned this wonderful early patent of a horse-drawn picker. John was asked how big the horse would have to be to pull such a machine, and John made a gesture on his chest. The judge asked John how tall he was. The New York lawyer for CRCO questioned the judge on any relevance to how tall John Strait was. The judge replied, "If you're going to use Prof. Strait as a measuring stick, I want to know how tall he is." Second, John was being questioned about the speed of revolution of the picking reel of the prior art. Since patents are not to scale, John and CRCO's lawyer had to agree on certain dimensions, gear ratios, etc., to compute the speed of the reel. The patented reel was very fast, I believe 1800 rpm. John Strait had mentioned a certain gear ratio, and the lawyer corrected him, suggesting a different ratio. John readily agreed and computed the speed; this horse-drawn machine had a reel speed of 1800 rpm, identical to CRCO's machine. We had worked through this computation prior to trial and had arrived at a very workable speed, not identical to CRCO but satisfactory. When CRCO's attorney made the ratio change, which John agreed to, the speeds came out identical.

CRCO's expert gave a very rehearsed testimony on direct examination. This was quite obvious. This changed when he was questioned on cross-examination about certain tests of John Ward's prototype—his face lit up, he departed from his script and testified, "Did we pick rocks? Those bags of beans are only supposed to weigh about twenty pounds. I bet they weighed over one-hundred-fifty pounds." (These weights are only an example; I don't recall the actual weights involved.)

CRCO had one of their machines in the courthouse parking area, and next to it, we had a Paulson Bros. machine. One trial day, we all trooped to the parking area for the court to view the machines. The court reporter was there, but I don't know how much was transcribed. The twins were all over the judge, pointing out first one thing and then another, which made their machine significantly different from CRCO's machine. We concluded this very satisfactory (from our standpoint) demonstration of the two machines with the judge asking specifically for certain photographs of a part of the machine, which made no sense to me; it caused me to worry about the judge's understanding of our case.

Judge Stone found that the defendants had presented clear and convincing evidence that both patents in the suit were invalid and that the plaintiff had failed to prove infringement of claim 1 of the John Ward patent, 2,675,663.

The decision of Judge Stone is reported at 187 F.Supp.489, 127 USPQ 124 (W.D. WI, 1960).

Two post trial events: Judge Stone, believing that the plaintiff would appeal, which did not happen, mailed to me current decisions of the Seventh Circuit, which he thought would help me win any appeal.

Paulson Brothers Industries went on to great success, building bigger and bigger machines until they overextended themselves, ran into financial trouble, and were bought out by the Chisholm Ryder Company. Subsequently, we were asked to do patent work for CRCO.

One further aside. This case took me to California to investigate prior art bean pickers. I don't remember too much of my trip except I had been north of LA and was driving to a point south of LA on Memorial Day weekend. I was on the freeway at a junction of several freeways. Traffic was so slow, I thought I was going to run out of gas on the freeway in the middle of a huge traffic jam. Another interesting topic among some local people was the price of the land where Disneyland was built, which they should have bought before Disney did. Of course, the value of the land had skyrocketed.

CHARLES W. HANSEN V. SIEBRING

Hansen had sued Siebring for patent infringement, and Siebring entered into a consent decree of validity and infringement of U.S. Patent 2,867,314 on a bunk feeder for farm animals. The feeder was made up of a feed hopper and an elongated discharge or delivery tube mounted on a frame. The tube was in sections, with one end mounted to the hopper. An auger was disposed within the tube, and the turning of the auger caused feed from the hopper to be discharged through longitudinally spaced holes in the delivery tube. The holes in the tube were progressively lower from a high point adjacent the hopper to a low point at the outer end of the tube. By means of a tube rotation control lever, the tube could be rotated to adjust feed through the holes. The function of this invention was to provide even distribution of feed along the length of the tube into a bunk feeder for the animals.

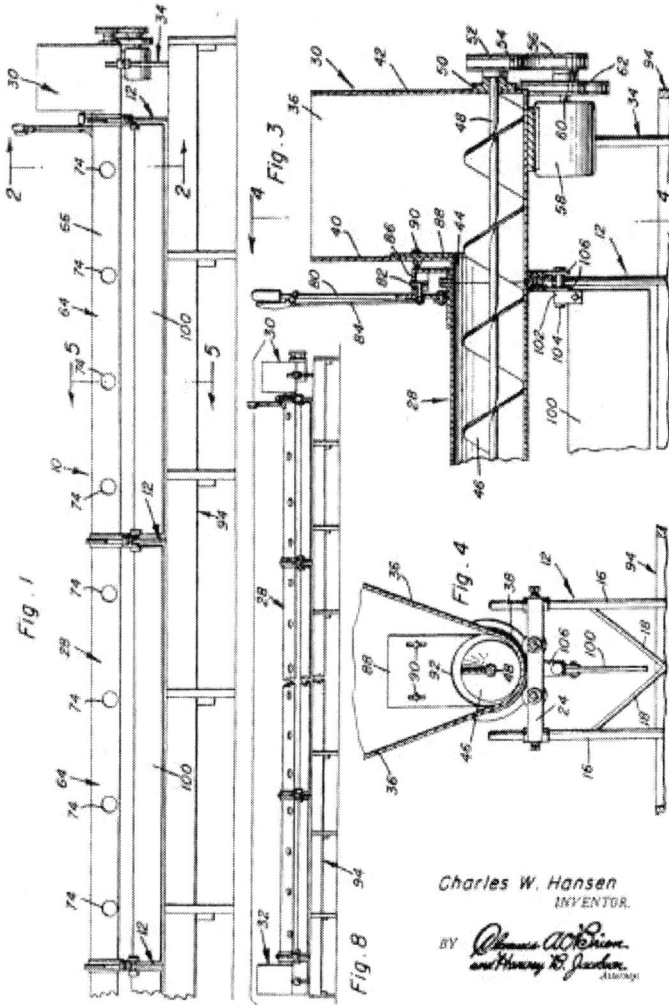

Jan. 6, 1959

C. W. HANSEN

AUGER CONVEYOR

2,867,314

Filed June 18, 1957

2 Sheets-Sheet 1

Charles W. Hansen
INVENTOR.

The consent decree provided for an injunction, and shortly after its entry, the defendants continued to manufacture and sell an infringing product. The suit was for contempt of the prior injunction because the defendants' modified bunk feeder was only colorably different from the enjoined product. At the defendants' insistence, although not an issue of the complaint, the court also decided the issue of infringement with respect to three variations in the defendants' product.

The trial was before District Judge Hanson in the Northern District of Iowa. Phil Smith was with me and aided in the trial. At a preliminary hearing, the judge pulled me aside to advise that my associate at an earlier hearing should never tell the court when it should make its decision. "The court will make its decision when it is ready to do so." The trial was interesting to me for several reasons. First, there was an interruption of the trial so the court could attend a conference. Upon returning, our first day was a very long one—lasting until 6:00 or 6:30 PM. The next day, the defendants' counsel had concluded direct examination of their expert about 5:30 PM. I thought it was a good point to recess for the day, and I told the court this. "Judge, we should finish this case by noon tomorrow."

The judge looked at me and said, "We're going to finish this case today; proceed, gentlemen."

About 6:30 or 7:00 PM, I said to the court, "Aren't we going to recess for dinner?"

The judge looked at me and said, "Yes, Mr. Gould, I can see you are hungry. We'll recess an hour for dinner."

Hungry? I was about to die of exhaustion! We did finish the case that day, at probably 10:30 or 11:00 PM.

Fairly early in the trial, I had spent an afternoon cross-examining Owen Siebring, the son and codefendant with his father, Claude Siebring. At the end of that day, Owen was still under cross-examination. He came to me and said he wanted to settle. He did not want to go back on that stand the next morning. I told him that I couldn't talk to him, that he should talk to his lawyer and have his lawyer get in touch with me. The lawyer did so and advised that any settlement would have to be approved by the father. The next morning, it was reported that the trial would have to proceed. The father appreciated Owen's concern but said any settlement would have to be approved by Owen's sister, who also had an interest in Siebring Manufacturing Company. The sister refused to settle. Owen told me that if she didn't want to settle, she could get up there on the witness stand in place of him. This didn't happen, and poor Owen had to go back under cross-examination that morning. The favorable decision by the district judge is reported at 231 F. Supp. 634. Phil Smith argued the appeal. The District Court was affirmed, 346 F2d 474 (8th Cir. 1965). The court not only found Siebring in contempt of the prior consent decree, but at the urging of the defendants, also found the defendants' bunk feeders to infringe the Hansen Patent. The court awarded costs, disbursements, and attorneys' fees.

AMERICAN INFRA-RED RADIANT CO. AND HUPP CORP. V. LAMBERT INDUSTRIES INC.

Our client was Agard Lambert of Virginia, Minnesota, and his company, Lambert Industries. This was a suit by American Infra-Red Radiant Co. and Hupp Corp. for infringement of two U.S. patents, U.S. Patent 2,775,294 and 2,870,830. The subject of the suit was infrared gas burners. The '294 patent related to the ceramic plate of the burner, and the '830 patent related to the burner housing, exclusive of the ceramic burner plate.

Dec. 25, 1956   G. SCHWANK   2,775,294

RADIATION BURNERS

FIG. 3

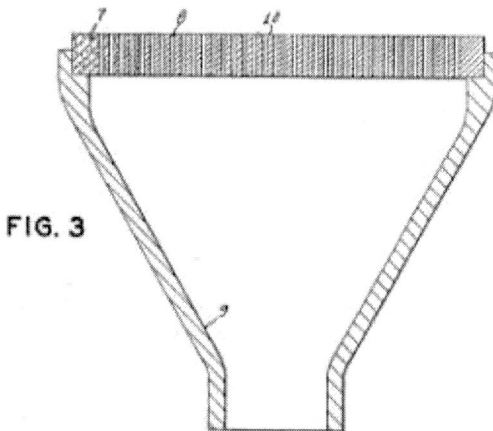

The suit was started in 1962 or early 1963. I can't recall much about the case prior to the fall of 1963. I had filed Letters Rogatory for response in Germany. American Infrared was the assignee of the patents from the inventor, Gunther Schwank of Germany, and Hupp Corp. was a nonexclusive licensee with a right to sue for infringement. I was waiting for the responses to the Letters Rogatory for many months, so I had done little to prepare the case for trial. Immediately upon receiving the answers to the Letters Rogatory in late 1963, I also received a notice of trial of the case at the January term in Duluth, Minnesota. I called counsel for plaintiffs to obtain consent to continue the case to the next term. They would not agree to continue the case but told me they would not object if I brought a motion to continue the case. I filed the motion for a hearing in early January 1964. At the hearing before Chief Judge Edward Devitt, the plaintiffs' counsel strongly objected to a continuance, and Judge Devitt denied my motion. I talked to the judge after his ruling to get time to prepare the case for trial, and he told me to talk to Judge Donovan, the Duluth judge assigned to the case. I talked to Donovan, and he advised that, in view of Judge Devitt's denial of a continuance, there was not much he could do to help me except put a large admiralty case he had to try ahead of our case on the calendar.

Bob Edell from Honeywell's patent department had just joined M&G on January 2, 1964. Bob was eager to get into litigation, although he was not yet admitted to practice. I called Bob from Duluth to advise him to get ready, as we were going to trial in the Lambert case.

At the time I called Bob, I had no expert witnesses for the case. With Bob's help, we obtained the services of Tom Carson, an electrical and gas engineer with the gas company; Charles Twine, an expert on ceramics; and Fred Lange, a practicing patent lawyer with the Dorsey firm. The case went to trial about mid-May, so from January 15, 1964, to May 15, 1964, Bob and I got this case ready for trial. We had a number of tests with gas burners. The only pretrial experience of note that I recall was Agard Lambert driving from Virginia, Minnesota, with a tank of acetylene gas in his trunk. Tom Carson was appalled when he heard this because of the volatility of acetylene gas. Carson thought it fortunate that Lambert didn't get blown up with that gas tank bouncing around in his truck.

The trial took place in Duluth. We brought several gas burners into court along with tanks of LP gas. We also had a microscope for viewing the ceramic plates. At the beginning of the trial, Bob and I brought a motion to add a complaint for violation of the antitrust laws. This was granted. The plaintiffs put on their first witness, who testified on the commercial success of the invention. Upon conclusion of his testimony, Bill Strauch, senior counsel for the plaintiffs, told the court, "Plaintiffs rest." I froze, wondering what to do. Should I rest? The plaintiffs had put in no evidence of infringement. In contemplating what I should do, I missed all of the excitement behind me. The plaintiffs' lawyers and witnesses were sitting in the jury box, and Neale, a partner of Strauch, vaulted the jury box rail, rushed up to Bill Strauch, and whispered in his ear. Bill Strauch then advised the court of his error. He meant to say, "Plaintiffs are through with this witness."

At that point, Judge Donovan, while erasing his "plaintiffs rest" notation, commented, "Well, in these patent cases, one never knows because plaintiffs rely on their presumption of validity." Neale promptly took over trying the case for the plaintiffs.

The plaintiffs had a consulting engineer, Clarence Fishleigh, as an expert witness on infringement. He had prepared the most beautiful charts I had ever seen: large colored charts with the elements of the claims broken down, pictures of the parts of the defendant's alleged infringing products, and text demonstrating how the elements of each claim read on the defendant's products. These charts were very impressive exhibits.

Our best prior art to prove invalidity was the McCourt patent. The plaintiffs had ceramic tiles made in accordance with the McCourt patent and were introducing extensive test results on the McCourt patent through a Hupp Corporation supervisor of the tests. I objected on foundation because he had not performed the actual tests. The objection was sustained, and Hupp Corporation returned with the person who had conducted the tests as their witness. On voir dire, I was about to demonstrate that this witness also could not lay a proper foundation when Edell grabbed me by the coattail and whispered, "John, we need these tests in evidence for support on the McCourt patent." So, I magnanimously advised the court that we had "no objection to the exhibit."

We put on a great trial. Some events I recall:

Donovan would repeatedly advise counsel to approach the bench. Thinking this at first to be a matter of some consequence, we discovered it was only the judge sharing a joke with us. I have no idea what the parties thought of these frequent conferences with the judge at his bench.

As part of our case, we were demonstrating "flashback" to the court. Upon a gas burner exhibiting flashback on ignition, there is a very loud noise. I advised the court what was going to happen. But when the flashback occurred, Judge Donovan leaped so in his chair, I thought we were going to have to scrape him off the ceiling.

The court and all counsel viewed the various ceramic tiles through a microscope. We trooped in a line to do this. I have difficulty focusing a microscope, and I'm sure Judge Donovan saw nothing in this demonstration. We filed extensive printed briefs before the district court: defendants' main reply brief on patent issues, defendants' brief on counterclaim, defendants' reply brief on patent validity issues, and defendants' reply brief on antitrust counterclaim.

We received a favorable decision by Judge Donovan, in which he found both patents valid but not infringed. Reported at 238 F. Supp. 176 (D. Mn. 1965), the court found "… that the patents in suit, as compared to defendants' accused device, are so substantially dissimilar in thought, construction, form, and performance as to require a finding in fact and law as not constituting infringement in the present case. I so hold."

The court's opinion provided that findings of fact, conclusions of law, and order for and form of judgment consistent with the foregoing may be presented in the court on February 19, 1965, at 10 AM.

Bob and I worked very hard preparing findings of fact and conclusions of law consistent with the court's opinion of no infringement. We were able to prepare detailed findings, which we felt would be sustained on appeal. I was concerned that at the hearing on the 19th, the plaintiffs' counsel would present the court with their gas burner and the defendants' gas burner and say, "Judge, don't look at the labels, but which is whose burner?" Bear in mind that the judge had found the two burners so different in thought, form, and construction.

The plaintiffs' counsel tried to present and argue findings of infringement, but Judge Donovan was very firm and told the plaintiffs' counsel he would only enter findings of fact and conclusions of law consistent with his opinion. He signed our proposed findings, conclusions, and order as prepared by us without amendment or change.

The case was appealed to the Eighth Circuit. The plaintiffs appealed the court's finding of no infringement, Appeal No. 18054; we appealed the court's finding of validity and the dismissal of our counterclaim for violation of the antitrust laws, Appeal No. 18055.

In Appeal No. 18054, we filed a brief for defendants-appellees, which supported the detailed findings of fact of no infringement. In Appeal No. 18055, we filed a brief for defendants-appellants; the plaintiffs filed their reply brief for plaintiffs-appellees; and we filed a reply brief for defendants-appellants. The appeal was argued before

Chief Judge Vogel and Circuit Judges Blackmun and Gibson. Judge Gibson wrote the opinion reported at 360 F.2d 977 (8th Cir. 1966).

In a very detailed opinion, the court found the Schwank U.S. Patent 2,775,294 invalid for want of "novelty," and even if novel, found the patent certainly lacked the necessary "invention." Because of its finding of invalidity, the question of infringement was rendered moot and not discussed by the court.

> In arriving at its decision, the court stated, "… From the statements of plaintiffs' own expert witnesses, and from the admission found in plaintiffs' supplemental brief,Note 3,that the Schwank patent has been anticipated in all ways save the possibility of one, this one being Schwank's teaching of a ratio of not less than 'about 20 percent' while McCourt's patent lists ratios of only 14.3 percent and 16.2 percent. Our task then is to determine if this single difference found in the stated ratios … entitles Schwank to a patent monopoly on his burner plate. We do not believe that it does."

With appropriate humility, I must confess my cross-examination of the plaintiffs' experts was superb.

In arguing to the Eighth Circuit, I remember stating that the only difference between the McCourt prior art and the Schwank burner tile was a 5 percent difference in the number of holes. The court reminded me that my math was wrong. The difference between 20 percent and 15 percent was not 5 percent. It seems like a 5 percent difference to me, but undoubtedly, the court's clerk had provided the court with a different formula.

The main issue with respect to U.S. Patent 2,870,830 ('830) was its invalidity under 35 USC Sec. 102(d). The crucial issue on this point was whether a German Gebrauchsmuster was a patent within the meaning of 102(d). I believe this to be a case of first impression. The Eighth Circuit stated, "There are no judicial cases indicating how a Gebrauchsmuster should be treated under the provisions of 102(d), and only scant authority as to how Gebrauchsmusters are to be treated under other provisions of our patent law."

We also had very good arguments of no infringement of the '830 patent, and the Eighth Circuit held that even if the '830 patent were valid, the plaintiffs had not borne their burden of proving infringement.

On our counterclaim for violation of the antitrust laws, added at the last moment, the court of appeals recognized the abstract possibility that the contractual arrangements of the plaintiffs, in their totality, might come into conflict with the antitrust law; however, the court affirmed the trial court on our failure to produce any concrete evidence of monetary damage.

This case was also memorable because Mary and I had rented a cottage on Cape Cod near Truro for two weeks in July. We had planned a leisurely drive out to visit Mary's sister in Michigan. The trial went on and on for six weeks. I think our station wagon was packed with our four boys sitting in it for a week waiting for me.

We must have finished the second of July. I remember I had to go into the office for at least one day, and we left for Cape Cod on the fourth of July. We had a great vacation that summer. Our cabin was very close to the Bay side, but once the boys were in the ocean, our swimming changed to the ocean side, which was not far away. The Cape gets very narrow at Truro.

Nineteen sixty-four was an eventful year. My mother died, after our vacation, later that year at the age of sixty-four.

1965

1965 was a very busy year for me. The court in *Ski-Mate Co. v. Western Auto Supply Co*, 245 F. Supp. 713 (S.D. Texas, 1965) rendered its decision in my favor on June 24, 1965. This case involved water ski bindings. Our client was Ron-Vik Inc. of Minneapolis. The defendant, Western Auto, was a customer of Ron-Vik. With respect to this case, I got to know Tom Arnold of Houston, Texas. He was our local counsel.

The case was not tried, but on stipulation of the parties, it was submitted to the court upon the pleadings, stipulations, answers to requests for admissions and interrogatories, and discovery depositions. Although the court found the patent valid, it found no infringement. The plaintiff admitted no literal infringement, but asserted infringement under the doctrine of equivalents. I have no recollection of the depositions in this case or the time period I worked on the case. My time records do not go back that far. We had very good arguments of no infringement, and the court's decision reflects this.

The following two cases, the Malco case and the Nortronics case were also tried in 1965.

MALCO MANUFACTURING COMPANY V. NATIONAL CONNECTOR CORPORATION

This case came to us from Leonard Lindquist of Lindquist & Vennum. The suit was commenced on September 14, 1961, for infringement of U.S. Patents 2,995,617, 3,086,074, and 3,136,591. The subject matter generally was electrical connectors used in automatic wire wrapping of the terminals in printed circuit boards. I am not sure when Bob Edell and I tried this case. It was prior to my trial in the Nortronics case discussed hereinafter. Judge Devitt's decision in the Nortronics case is dated September 29, 1965. Although Judge Nordbye's decision in the National Connector Case is dated September 13, 1966, I am guessing that we tried that case in the spring of 1965.

Aug. 8, 1961   P. A. MAXIMOFF ET AL   2,995,617

SELF-LOCKING TERMINAL

Filed Nov. 3, 1958   3 Sheets—Sheet 1

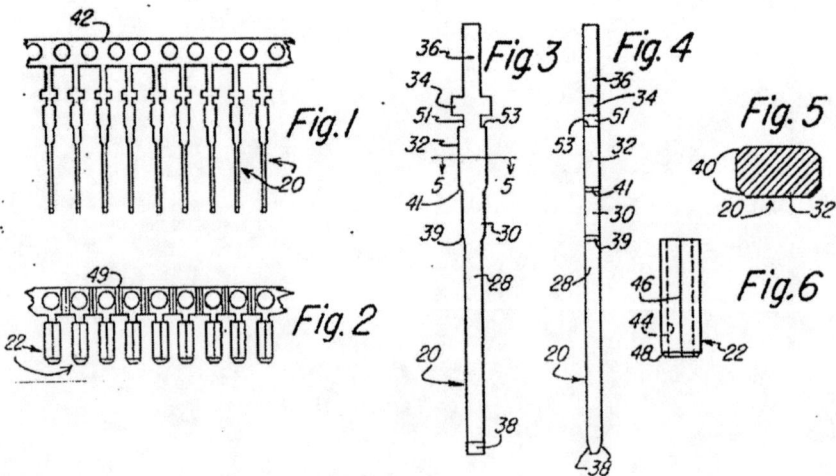

April 16, 1963   A. JUST ET AL   3,086,074

SELF-ORIENTATING TERMINAL CONNECTORS

Filed Feb. 13, 1961

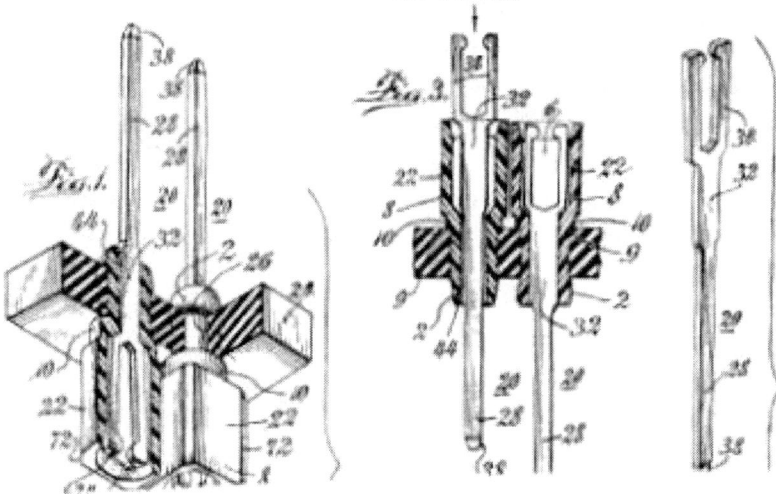

Several of the defendant's connectors were in suit, identified as Types A–F. I've forgotten which type was sold by the defendant primarily to the government.

Unfortunately, National Connector had made a few sales of their government-style connector to others than the U.S. government, which gave the plaintiff jurisdiction over this style of connector in this case. To satisfy the government's specifications, National Connector's drawings were identical to Malco's drawings in every dimension. It was grueling to listen to the plaintiff's witness going through every dimension of National's connector and comparing such with Malco's drawings. Another memorable trial moment was watching a video introduced by the plaintiff showing NASA's space craft lifting off. This successful launch was, according to the plaintiff, the direct result of using printed circuit boards with the plaintiff's terminal connectors.

With three patents and five different connectors in suit, it was quite a trial. Opposing counsel were William Marshall Lee and Roy Hofer of the Hume firm in Chicago. They were very competent and tough. Judge Nordbye, in his decision, reported at 151 USPQ 255 (D. Minn. 1966), found Claims 1, 2, 3, 5, 6, 7 and 9 of the '617 patent valid and that the defendant's Type A and B terminal connectors infringed. The Type C connector was found not to infringe. The court found claims 1–4 of U.S. Patent 3,086,074 to be invalid and therefore not infringed. The court found claims 1 and 2 of U.S. Patent 3,136,591 invalid but not by reason of a sale more than one year before the filing date of the application resulting in the '591 patent.

Judge Nordbye, in his finding of fact 23, quoted what he found to be the heart of the plaintiffs' novelty in the '617 patent, and which he found the defendant, in its Type A and B connectors, infringed.

On appeal, in our brief for defendant-appellant, we started our argument on the fact that Judge Nordbye found the claim language "gripping shank having a minimum transverse dimension" referred to the locking notches in the pin. Since the court found the defendant did not have this element in the form of locking notches, we argued that the trial court had to eliminate this element from the claim to find infringement of the heart of the plaintiffs' invention. We further argued that if a summary of the invention was to be used to determine infringement, then the same summary, containing the same elements, must be used to determine validity. We then pointed out, in argument and charts attached to our brief, how each element of the heart of the plaintiffs' invention was in the prior art.

We had other very good arguments on appeal. We argued that the trial court had placed undue emphasis on the plaintiffs' alleged commercial success. We mentioned that the volume of testimony by plaintiffs on alleged commercial success ballooned the issue out of proportion to its importance in the case. Note prior reference to the video of NASA's space craft launch.

Judge Nordbye was a very highly respected Judge. He was seldom reversed by the Eighth Circuit. The appeal was argued by me for the defendant and Bill Marshall for the plaintiffs before Circuit Judges Vogel, Blackmun and Lay. The Eighth Circuit Opinion is reported at 392 F.2d 766 (8th Cir. 1968). Basically, the court found the '617 patent invalid as being obvious under 35 U.S.C. Sec. 103.

The plaintiffs filed a petition for certiorari to the Supreme Court of the U.S. We opposed this petition with a brief in opposition, and certiorari was denied on October 28, 1968 (see 159 USPQ 799). We apparently brought a further motion before Judge Nordbye to permit us to present evidence that the defendant was entitled to reasonable attorneys fees. This motion was granted on February 24, 1969, 163 USPQ 22; however, I have no recollection or record of the result. Perhaps it settled out.

MICHIGAN MAGNETICS INC. V. THE NORTRONICS COMPANY

We represented the defendant, Nortronics, a manufacturer of magnetic heads. The suit was for infringement of U.S. Patent 2,835,742. It was commenced on November 2, 1961.

May 20, 1958   W. D. MOEHRING ET AL   2,835,742

MAGNETIC HEAD FOR RECORDER AND REPRODUCER

Filed Nov. 8, 1954

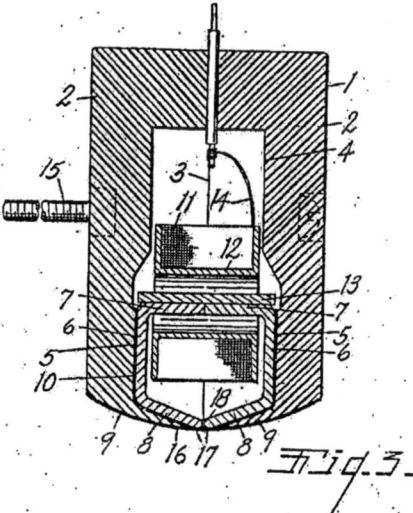

Fig. 3.

This case was very important to the defendant because most of its production of magnetic heads would be affected by an adverse decision. We did not have the litigating manpower we have today. I went to the firm of Schroeder, Siegfried & Ryan to get Joe Ryan as an expert for me in the case. Joe deferred, but Ken Siegfried said he would be able to help me prepare the case for trial. What a mistake.

As I mentioned above in discussing the *Malco v. National Connector* case, I was in trial before Judge Nordbye when Judge Devitt informed me that he was ready to try the Nortronics case as soon as I finished the National Connector case. As Judge Nordbye said in his memorandum decision, the National Connector case had many issues in a "lengthy and involved patent litigation." I went to see Judge Devitt after finishing the National Connector Case to discuss continuing the Nortronics Case to give me time to recover. I told Judge Devitt that I was exhausted, and it would not be fair to my client, Nortronics, to go right into trying another case. His reply: "Don't give me that bullshit, John. You're going to trial." I've forgotten the details, but he did give me a couple of weeks respite.

I gave Ken Siegfried the job of preparing an employee of Nortronics to testify about Nortronics manufacturing procedures; in particular, that the ends of the magnetic cores and the case halves were not finished in "common flat planes" in Nortronics' magnetic heads. This witness, whose name escapes me, decided he was to be our star witness. Ken had really prepared him, and Ken was to conduct this witness' testimony. The night before he was to testify, I cross-examined him, and he changed his testimony three times. I met with Leonard Kronfeld, the president of Nortronics, and in spite of the fact that I had told Judge Devitt this witness would be on the stand the next morning, I told Leonard Kronfeld that no way would this witness take the stand. Instead, I prepared Kronfeld to bring in the evidence we needed. I've forgotten just how I provoked a disagreement with opposing counsel on stipulating to certain evidence in court the next morning, but I told Judge Devitt that in view of the plaintiff's failure to stipulate, I was not going to call the witness prepared by Ken Siegfried. I will give Ken Siegfried credit for preparing some great charts exhibiting our prior art, but his aid in trying the case was nonexistent.

My cross–examination of the plaintiff's inventor, Mr. Murphy, on the prior art prompted Judge Devitt to question the witness himself. When asked to explain what features of his invention were important, Mr. Murphy referred to providing a magnetic coil around the rear legs of the core pieces.

The Court: Didn't you say that was old in the Shure Bros. head?

Mr. Murphy: Yes.

The Court: Any other feature important?

Mr. Murphy referred to another alleged feature of the invention, and the court again said:

The Court: Wasn't that old in other prior art?
Mr. Murphy: Yes.

I cannot seem to find the transcript in this case. But I recall Mr. Murphy was reduced to telling the court that their invention was a new combination of admittedly old elements. The defendant's brief filed after trial points out:

"Indeed, Mr. Murphy, when questioned by the court, could not testify to any specific features of the patent in suit, not known in the Eckert patent or Shure Bros. head."

In addition to invalidity, we had good arguments of no infringement. Mr. Kronfeld, not Ken's witness, testified that the defendant's differential lapping technique provided that the pole tips protruded beyond any adjacent core material a distance of approximately twenty millionths of an inch. A witness for the plaintiff had testified on cross that a difference between the plane of the core tips and the core holder material of ten millionths of an inch meant they wouldn't be in the same plane, as required by the claims.

Judge Devitt didn't involve himself in the details of millionths of inches but rendered the issue of infringement moot by holding the patent claims invalid.

Judge Devitt's opinion is reported at 245 F. Supp.401 (D. Minn. 1965).

Shortly after this trial, Leonard Kronfeld's only son died unexpectedly. This was devastating for Leonard. He was Jewish but not very religious. I recall visiting Leonard and expressing, probably for the first time to anyone, my own belief in a loving God and in a life after death. We talked a long time, and I think it was of comfort to Leonard.

TRUVAL SHIRT COMPANY INC. V. TARGET STORES INC.

This was one of the few trademark cases that I tried. I believe most trademark cases should settle unless considerable damages are involved. Paul Welter second chaired me in this trial. The plaintiff was represented by Curtis Roy of the Dorsey firm.

The case was for trademark infringement and unfair competition brought by a New York shirt manufacturer against Target stores for using the trademark "Tarval" on shirts. The plaintiff's registered trademark was "Truval."

The case was a three-day bench trial, and I recall very little about the case except that it required considerable effort not to confuse the names during the trial.

With Paul Welter's good help, we were able to put on a really good case. The mark "Tarval" was chosen following a contest by Target and is a combination of the words "target" and "value." We were able to show good faith in the adoption of the name. We also pointed out that "Truval" was a relatively weak mark derived from the words "true" and "value." We were also able to show that the channels of trade or methods of merchandizing the shirts were different. Target's shirts were sold on a self-service basis at its several Target stores. The court was impressed that there was little likelihood of confusion by a discount store shopper thus obligated to make his own examination and appraisal of the merchandise.

The plaintiff put on considerable evidence of its extensive advertising. I recall the plaintiff's witness going into several publications of *Playboy* and *Esquire* magazines. We, of course, did not look at the pictures. We countered this evidence by a survey that demonstrated that the level of awareness of "Truval" shirts in the Twin Cities was very low.

The court concluded no likelihood of confusion and no unfair competition. Judgment for the defendant. The case was not appealed and is reported as *Truval Shirt Co. Inc. v. Target Stores Inc.* 259 F. Supp. 151, 151 USPQ 311 (D. Mn. 1966).

As an aside, it is my understanding that Judge Devitt's decision was later criticized in a publication.

BRITT TECH CORP. ET AL. V. L&A PRODUCTS INC. AND JAMES F. LINDSAY

L&A Products and Jim Lindsay were represented by a well-known St. Paul lawyer, Dick Leonard, and by a St. Paul patent attorney, John Stryker. When this case was about a month from trial, I was asked by Dick Leonard to take over the trial of the case. I was told that it was a very clear case of no infringement. I told Mr. Leonard that I might be able to take it on if no infringement was clear and to get me information about the case. I reviewed the matter, and at a meeting with Mr. Lindsay and Dick Leonard, I advised them that the issue of infringement was not as clear as I had been told and that I would be able to handle the case only if Judge Nordbye granted a continuance of the trial. I brought a motion before Judge Nordbye to continue the trial to give me time to properly prepare the case for trial. Judge Nordbye denied the motion on the grounds that "John Gould isn't the only good patent lawyer in town. Get someone else to try the case, if Mr. Gould is so busy." So, the case was tried and lost by Dick Leonard. I was hired to handle the appeal.

Oct. 16, 1962   O. B. HARMES ET AL   3,058,668
CLEANING APPARATUS

Filed Oct. 7, 1960   4 Sheets—Sheet 1

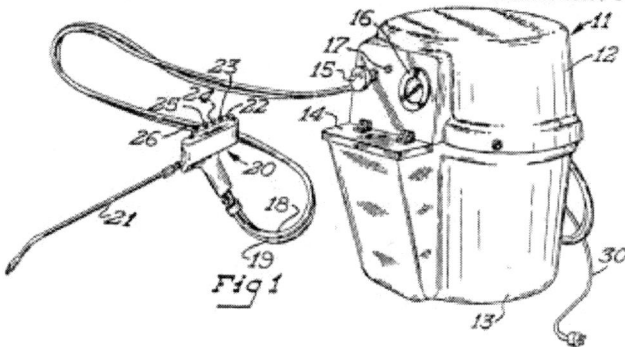

Fig 1

The trial record in this case was not very helpful. Although the necessary prior art had been introduced into evidence, it had not been used very effectively. Paul Welter and I put together some fourteen diagrams attached as an appendix to our appellants' brief, showing in simplified form the plaintiff's patented pressure washer equipment, L&A's alleged infringing pressure washer, the prior art Ackerman carwashing apparatus, the Wyatt prior art machine, and a Wyatt-Ackerman combination machine. Our diagrams reflected two important phases of the equipment: the soap phase and the rinse phase. None of these diagrams were exhibits at trial, but they were demonstrative of the exhibits that were in evidence.

As previously mentioned, Judge Nordbye was a very highly respected District Court judge, not very often reversed by the Eighth Circuit. We were helped in two respects. First, Judge Nordbye had found that the heart of the plaintiff's invention was a solenoid restrictor valve in the water line. Without defining what a "restrictor valve" was, Judge Nordbye found the defendants had appropriated the heart of the plaintiff's invention.

You will recall that Judge Nordbye had used this "heart of the invention" theory in the National Connector case.

Our main argument was that the patent claims must be given the same interpretation on the issue of validity as on the issue of infringement. If the claims were given the same broad interpretation on validity as on the issue of infringement, the claims were invalid.

Second, the U.S. Supreme Court had recently decided the trilogy of cases including *Graham v. John Deere*. The trial court had appeared to equate novelty with patentability and had not made the factual inquiries required by Graham and had not determined the obviousness or non-obviousness of the invention.

So, Paul Welter and I ignored the trial record in this case and wrote a great appellants' brief—and, of course, I must have made a great argument before the Eighth Circuit. Judge Nordbye's decision was reversed; the patent was held invalid "on the intervening authority of *Graham's* guidelines." This case is reported at 365 F.2d 83 (8th Cir. 1966). See the great diagrams in the appendix to our brief. An example is below.

WYATT-ACKERMAN Combination
Soap Phase

DIAGRAM-11

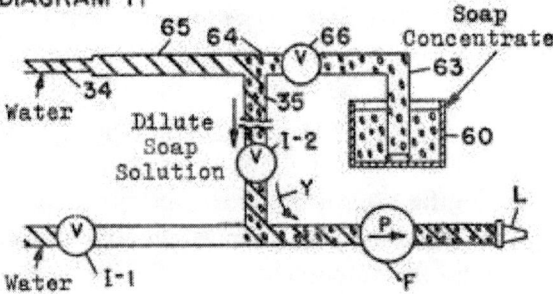

The Alleged Infringing Device
Soap Phase

DIAGRAM-12

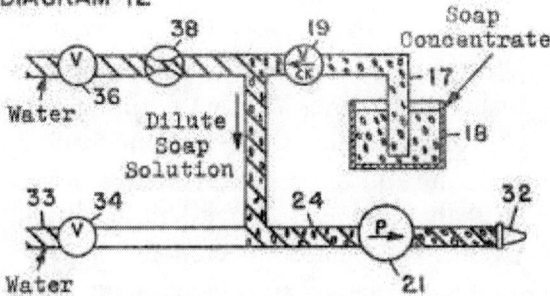

FARMHAND INC. V. CRAVEN

This was the first of three lawsuits I tried for Farmhand on the invention of Boyd Schiltz of a chain-type haystack mover. The trial of this case was a *trial*. First, the case was originally scheduled to take place a year earlier. As was customary, Bob Edell and I arrived in Aberdeen, South Dakota, a few days before trial; we learned at the last minute that the case was to be postponed. It was almost a year later, when we were again in Aberdeen for the trial, that we learned that the defendant's mother had died.

We went to a scheduled pretrial set for hearing the morning of the day the trial was to start. Expecting the court to again postpone the trial because of the death of the defendant's mother, we went through the pretrial without any mention of the event. Finally, at the close of the pretrial, the defendant said, "Judge, you know my mother died."

The judge responded, "Yes, I know that."

The defendant asked, "Will I be able to take Wednesday afternoon off to be at my mother's funeral?"

The judge replied, "Yes, yes, of course."

As an aside, just before this trial, I had had a mental breakdown. I thought there was a conspiracy against me at the firm. Phil Smith and Edell, I thought, were plotting together to usurp my position in the firm. I went quite goofy. Maybe Mary can add something about this time. I was babbling to her, talking to my priest, etc. I believe I had a hearing in Minneapolis on some matter. I became quite incoherent, almost comatose on the way to the courthouse. My brother George was called, and I was hospitalized for several days. I remember thinking that the person in the bed next to me at the hospital was a spy. He was only there to spy on me. Fortunately, I was given appropriate medication, and I recovered. I remember that I was quite fearful of going back to the office, wondering how I would be perceived. Brother George gave me some good advice. He said, "Go back as though you are in charge of the firm." I did so, with much trepidation.

This trial was my first trial after my mental breakdown, and I wondered whether I could get through it. I did, but back to the trial.

Judge Beck of Aberdeen informed us at the pretrial that we would not need to make lengthy opening statements because he had just finished trying a patent case, and he knew all about them. I knew this to be wrong. The judge had just had a trademark case and not a patent case.

Half of each day of trial, I felt I was winning, and half of each day, I was losing. I had the defendant on the stand for cross-examination on Tuesday. The next morning, the judge, off the record, read the riot act to me. He was very abusive. He stated, "My clerk brought to my attention last evening that you are asking Mr. Craven the same questions you asked him at deposition."

I responded, "Yes, your Honor, I am putting this evidence into the trial record. The deposition is not in evidence."

The judge told me what I was doing was outrageous. "You are through with this witness." I responded by asking the court if I could at least ask the witness questions that I had not asked at his deposition. The judge gave me permission to do so. I moved the admission of the defendant's entire deposition into evidence, and then proceeded with further cross-examination of the defendant on the morning of his mother's funeral.

I had another battle with the judge during my examination of Prof. John Strait, our technical expert. Prof. Strait was testifying on how the claims read upon the defendant's haystack mover when he was interrupted by the judge: "I'm interested in the differences between the claims and Defendant's haystack mover; tell me what the differences are." Prof. Strait was in a difficult position because there were no differences. I've forgotten Prof. Strait's response, but the judge said to Mr. Strait, "I order you to tell me what the differences are." I had to intervene to protect Strait's testimony. I'm not sure how I did it, but I convinced Judge Beck that our burden was to show similarities and that the defendant had the burden to show what differences existed, if any. The judge relented in his order to Prof. Strait, and the trial proceeded. Don Sell, patent counsel for 3M, was our legal expert at this trial. In hindsight, I believe the judge was doing everything he could to prevent me from having a good trial record. In spite of—or maybe because of—my initial fear of going to this trial because of my mental breakdown, I persisted in at least making a trial record.

The defendant in this case had not pleaded invalidity, and the only issue was infringement. The court's opinion is reported at 324

F.Supp. 207(D. S.D. 1971). The court found no infringement based on the difference in the speed of the chains relative to the speed of the truck or trailer moving under the haystack. The haystacks weighed about twenty tons. The trailer or truck bed had a plurality of laterally spaced chains extending the length of the bed; drive means imparted concerted movement of the chains in a direction opposite to the direction imparted to the machine by its drive means at a rate on the incline such that the chain flights have a horizontal component of movement generally equal to the rate of machine movement. The court interpreted "generally equal" to include the inventor's specified speed of the chains being greater than the backward movement of the vehicle in the loading operation. Since Craven's chain speed was less than the backward movement of the vehicle, there was no infringement.

We appealed to the Eighth Circuit. I still have the appellant's brief, and it reads pretty well. The Eighth Circuit opinion was written by Judge Lay. It is reported at 455 F.2d 609 (8th Cir. 1972). At oral argument, I arranged two projectors, each with a short movie clip of the haystack movers in operation. One clip was of the patented machine, and the other was of the defendant's machine. This demonstration was very effective. Judge Lay held, "We think the overall record makes clear that the difference in the manner of operation of the two machines, if any exists at all, is merely one of degree."

Judge Lay, after his decision in this case, wrote an article on the effect of oral argument on appeal. I've looked for that article but can't find it at the moment. In his article, Judge Lay referred to my use of the movies in a patent case as a unique and effective oral argument. So, after a rocky start before Judge Beck, Boyd Schiltz's invention of a haystack mover was successfully litigated. Phil Smith wrote the patent application, but I take credit for inserting the broadening wording in claims 10 and 11 that the rate of chain speed was "generally equal" to the speed of vehicle movement. (See cover for image of the haystack mover.)

Before I get to the next trial of the haystack mover patent, I'll refer to two other cases.

HADFIELD V. RYAN EQUIPMENT CO.

This case was for an individual, Glen Hadfield. It was one of the most difficult cases I have tried, and it took a lot out of me personally. I vowed never to try another case for an individual client. Glen Hadfield was a difficult client. He was a large man, physically strong, stubborn, and somewhat uncontrollable. He had made a wonderful invention of an apparatus for automatically rolling up sod strips as the sod is being cut by the sod cutter. Until Hadfield's invention, laborers would follow the sod cutter, rolling the sod by hand. He started his own business manufacturing and selling attachments to be used with all of the then-commercial sod cutters, which converted them to be able to automatically roll up the sod. The Ryan Equipment Company of St. Paul, Minnesota, a large manufacturer of sod cutters, copied Glen Hadfield's invention, and we were hired to sue for patent infringement.

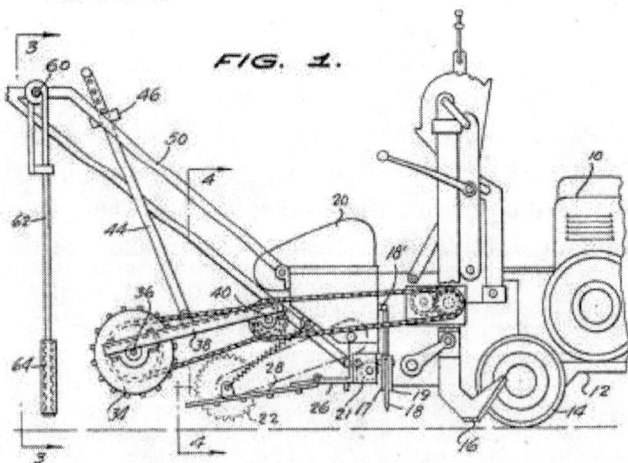

June 11, 1968   G. R. HADFIELD   3,387,666

FREEING, SEVERING AND ROLLING UP SOD

Filed Jan. 17, 1967   3 Sheets—Sheet 1

FIG. 1.

The only prior art to U.S. Patent 3,387,666 was a prior Hadfield patent, U.S. Patent 2,987,124, in which Glen included a drawing of a concept for rolling up sod. No machine was built according to this prior art concept until we had a prototype sample built to demonstrate that it would not function to produce the desired result of the patent in suit. Nevertheless, I was very troubled by this patent disclosure, and I recommended to Hadfield that he settle. I had taken the deposition of the president of Ryan Equipment Company, and he testified to his own company's efforts to build a machine that would automatically roll up the sod. His company's efforts were unsuccessful. Indeed, he testified at deposition: "I wish I had a nickel for every dollar I've spent trying to develop a machine to automatically roll sod." After this very successful deposition, the Ryan Equipment Company was willing to take a nonexclusive license and pay Hadfield a 10 percent royalty. I recommended that Hadfield accept the deal. He refused. He was making too much money selling attachments, and he wanted the Ryan Company out of the business as a competitor.

The Ryan Company's attorney took Hadfield's deposition. Unfortunately, he was not a good witness, and the Ryan Company received evidence that would help them at trial. This experience of Hadfield as a witness and my beating him over the head to settle finally convinced Hadfield to accept a 10 percent royalty license. I approached the Ryan Company's attorney with an offer to settle. It was too late. As a result of their deposition of Hadfield, they felt confident they would win and refused to settle.

The case was tried before Judge Nordbye. I was second chaired at the trial by Bob Edell. I was pleased that our judge was Judge Nordbye. I felt he was somewhat pro-patent and that he would favor the individual Hadfield against the corporate defendant. The defendant's main defense was that the patent was invalid over the combination of their prior art Ryan sod cutter with the parts disclosed in Hadfield's prior '124 patent. We had produced a movie showing the '124 concept wouldn't work to roll sod. Judge Nordbye asked for a demonstration of Hadfield's original prototype of his invention in suit. This prototype was brought in from Michigan, and we set up a demonstration in a sod field outside St. Paul. I wanted to engage a professional operator to operate the machine. Again, Hadfield refused. It was his invention; he would operate the machine. The demonstration was a disaster, and I'm sure it affected Judge Nordbye's decision. The patented machine didn't work any better than our movies of the unworkable '124 prior art. Judge Nordbye's decision was not reported, but he held the patent claims invalid as being obvious over the prior art of the Ryan sod cutter and Hadfield's prior art '124 patent. The fact that the '124 patent had been issued and was presumed to have utility and to be workable was a big factor against us. I asked Hadfield why he issued a worthless patent if he knew the '124 patent disclosure was unworkable. His reply: "I thought it was an honor to have the patent issued to me."

We appealed to the Eighth Circuit, and Judge Nordbye was affirmed. The decision is reported at 456 F.2d 1218 (8th Cir. 1972). The appellate hearing was held in St. Louis, and Hadfield brought a ton of relatives to St. Louis to hear my oral argument. After that hearing, Hadfield was so convinced that he would win the appeal, he put on a big celebratory dinner for me and all his relatives.

Hadfield had made a great invention. If tried today, with appeals to the Federal Circuit, his patent, I am convinced, would be held valid. In 1972, the Eighth Circuit had a reputation of being a graveyard for patents. Not many were ever found to be valid.

WILSON V. MIDWEST FOLDING PRODUCTS MFG. CORP.

This was a patent infringement suit in Chicago on Kermit Wilson's invention of folding table with individual chairs or stools. The patent in suit was U.S. Patent 3,055,705.

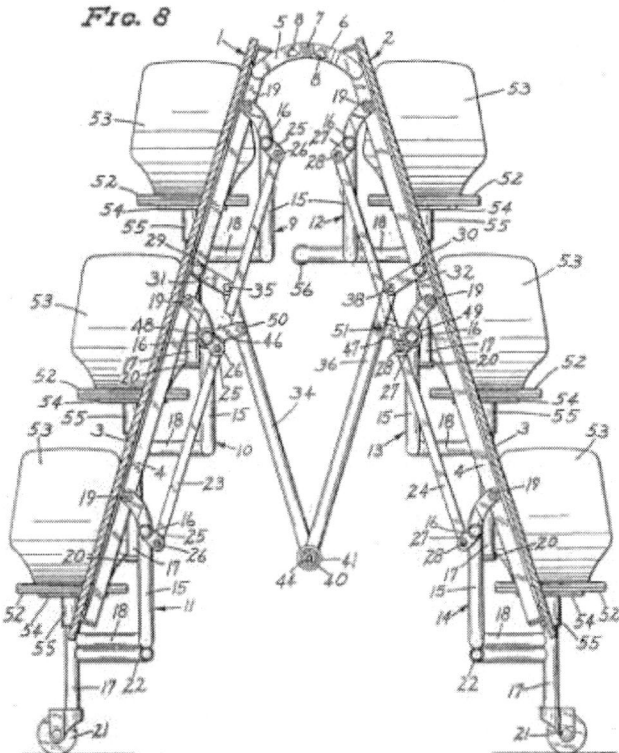

FIG. 8

If I recall correctly, this case was the first time I had occasioned metal detectors for entry into the courtrooms. We had several metal folding tables to get past the detectors and into the courtroom. We stayed in Chicago at the Union League Club, which was just kitty-corner from the federal courthouse. I remember wheeling these folding tables from the Union League Club into the courthouse. Kermit Wilson was present throughout the trial.

I don't know where the trial of this case went wrong. We really had a great invention with very little prior art. The defendant relied primarily upon U.S. Patent 2,788,059 to Mackintosh. Midwest Folding Products Mfg. Corp. made a model of this table, which was admitted to be a "modification" of the Mackintosh patent, and which was further modified with stools in an attempt to show its similarity to Wilson's patented table. The District Judge found the patent claims to be invalid as an obvious combination of old elements. Relying on the "rather severe test" of invention of the *A&P Tea Co. v. Supermarket Corp.*(1950)case by the U.S. Supreme Court, the court found Wilson's invention to be a combination of old elements, which would have been obvious to a person of ordinary skill in the art.

The court was convinced that any company that wanted to develop such a table could have done so by assigning the design task to its design and engineering personnel. The court failed to explain, if this were true, why it had not been done long before Kermit's invention.

We appealed this decision reported at 175 USPQ 649 to the Seventh Circuit, which affirmed Judge Tone's per curiam decision without a published opinion, 180 USPQ 547 (7th Cir. 1973). Judge Tone was a highly respected district judge later elevated to the Seventh Circuit Court of Appeals. We filed a petition for writ of certiorari to the Supreme Court, but the petition was denied, 181 USPQ 289 (1974).

This was a tough loss for me in an important case. Normally, when one loses such a case, the client takes his work to another firm. Kermit Wilson said to me, "John, you put on too good a case. The judge felt sorry for the defendant." Kermit was a wonderful client, and although he is now deceased, the firm continues to do work for his company, Sico Inc.

I may have mentioned the fact that Kermit Wilson was the partner of Henry Albrecht in the Waco case discussed above. Kermit had made an invention of a folding table, which he wanted to pursue commercially. Kermit sold his interest in Waco and started his own company, Seating Inc. The name later changed to Sico Inc. He had a pretty rough start, but Kermit was a great salesman with an outgoing and friendly personality. Kermit persisted and built a very successful company selling a variety of products to schools and hotels. He also established licensees in England and Asia.

Dick Flint of the Gray, Plant firm handled Sico's and Kermit's general legal matters. Both Dick and I have fond memories of our long relationship with Kermit Wilson. So, in spite of losing this case, I continued to do a lot of work for Sico and Kermit Wilson.

I remember that Kermit and I exchanged a lot of non-business (i.e., non-billable) correspondence. Kermit would clip items of interest concerning patents from various publications and send them to me, and I would clip items that I thought might interest Kermit and mail them to him. This is a way for young lawyers to develop and keep a good client relationship.

Perhaps this is good place to have an aside comment. When the firm was moving from our offices in the Midwest Plaza Building to the then–Norwest Center, I was told that archives wanted to get rid of several files of mine, so I had them sent to my office to look through. I was surprised to find how much correspondence I had developed as a very young lawyer, such as my correspondence with Kermit Wilson. I had kept in contact with law school classmates, who would later become important lawyers in major firms. This was a talent that as I got busier and the firm got busier I think got lost along the way. But I encourage this type of relationship to younger lawyers building a practice and building relationships.

COZY CAB MANUFACTURING V. CUSTOM PRODUCTS OF LITCHFIELD

Finally, getting back to some winning cases. I recall very little of this case. It was favorably settled after a partial trial. We represented the plaintiff, Cozy Cab. The suit was for breach of contract and unfair competition. The case was venued in U.S. District Court in Minnesota. I believe Paul Welter was helping me on this case. The main things I recall are that I had little time to prepare for this trial and that I worked over Memorial Day weekend—it was a hot weekend. We had our offices in the Midwest Plaza, and the air-conditioning was shut off for the holiday. I remember working in our library and suffering because of the temperature. The suit related to cabs built to be mounted on agricultural tractors.

FARMHAND INC. V. LAHMAN MFG. CO. INC.

This was my second trial involving Boyd Schiltz's invention of the haystack mover. Normally, this case would also have been brought in Aberdeen, South Dakota, the situs of my first trial. Because of the judge, we joined a customer of Lahman and brought the suit in Sioux Falls, South Dakota. The judge in Sioux Falls, because his fellow South Dakota judge in Aberdeen was familiar with the patent, in view of the Craven case, transferred the case to Aberdeen. Because of certain statements made by the trial judge in the Craven case, I believed him to be biased against Farmhand. I filed an affidavit of prejudice against the Aberdeen judge based on the record in the Craven case. I noted several biased comments, including one on the invalidity of the patent even though validity was not at issue. When an affidavit of prejudice is filed, the trial judge should take no further action in the case until the motion of prejudice is decided. Also, to dispose of such a motion, all a judge has to say is, "I'm not biased," and there is nothing a party can do about it. Well, we had a controversy concerning discovery, which the judge in Aberdeen set for hearing, without first deciding the issue of prejudice. Ken Siegfried, representing the defendant, and I arrived in Aberdeen for the hearing on the discovery matter. The judge came into the courtroom and announced he would hear the matter in chambers. This was not a good sign.

Ken and I settled ourselves at a table in the judge's chambers, and the judge, seated in his chair, announced, "In all my years as a federal judge, no one has ever filed an affidavit of prejudice against me." He pointed his finger at me and said, "What you did was beyond professional propriety." I've forgotten my response, but the judge, without deciding the prejudice issue, heard our discovery controversy. I remember going into a conference room with Ken to probably compromise the discovery issue, and I made careful notes of the judge's comments to me. Upon returning to Minneapolis, I filed a second affidavit of prejudice, and without comment, the judge recused himself.

So, the case was back in Sioux Falls, where it went to trial before Judge Nichol. Alan Carlson second chaired me in this case.

I have a transcript of the trial record in this case and copies of several of the briefs: plaintiff's main brief in the district court, plaintiff's reply brief in the district court, brief for plaintiff-appellee in the Eighth Circuit, reply brief for defendant-appellant, defendant's petition for writ of certiorari and appendix, and plaintiff's brief in opposition to the petition for certiorari.

Joe Maynes, a very competent general lawyer from Aberdeen, and Ken Siegfried, a patent lawyer from Minneapolis, tried the case for the defendant, and Alan Carlson and I tried the case for the plaintiff.

I do not have any clear recollection of war stories from this case except Joe Maynes's new exception to the hearsay rule. I haven't found it yet in the transcript (defendant's appendix on appeal). The exception: "Judge, we really need this."

We must have submitted pretrial briefs because the court in opening comments complimented both sides on the excellent trial briefs submitted. Judge Nichol had done his homework prior to trial to become familiar with patent law. As I briefly review the trial transcript, we put on a very good case. We started strong with a witness, James Seitz, a farmer since the age of fourteen. He had done custom haystack moving, both with the prior art cable-type movers and the Farmhand chain-type movers. He was able to testify to the importance of the invention in moving large haystacks. He was also familiar with Lahman's alleged infringing haystack mover, and he testified that its operation was not different from the Farmhand movers.

The inventor, Boyd Schiltz, testified. Defendant Fritz Lahman was called for adverse examination. We introduced testimony from several depositions. Don Sell, who became patent counsel for 3M, testified as our legal expert, and John Strait, professor of agricultural engineering at the University of Minnesota, testified as our technical expert.

The defendant introduced a mishmash of prior art to show the invention to have been obvious. The defendant gave notice of fourteen prior art patents, four prior inventors, and three persons with knowledge of a previously used invention. Two alleged prior art machines were the Rogers machine and the Sutton machine. We were able to use the Sutton machine testimony in our favor, as Sutton tried to make something easier to move haystacks than using cables, but his machine did not work. Mr. Rogers, a witness for the defense at trial, testified about his prior art machine. We had this to say about Rogers' prior art in our post trial brief:

> "It seems incredible … that Defendants have the audacity to ask the court to go even further than the oral uncorroborated testimony of Rogers and to 'modify (by hindsight) Rogers' tree-smashed piece of junk into a haystack mover in order to invalidate a meritorious invention."

The court, in its opinion, concluded that Rogers' oral testimony and the sketches based upon his recollection could be afforded little weight and that the Rogers machine could not be considered as prior art. With respect to Sutton, the court found: "After the initial unsuccessful attempt to get the machine to load a haystack, it was placed in various yards on the Sutton ranch, where it reposed until it was resurrected for this trial."

Judge Nichol, in his opinion decided September 27, 1976) 192 USPQ 749 (D. S.D. 1976, found the patent valid and infringed. The court wrote a very well-reasoned opinion following the guidelines of *Graham v. John Deere Co.* on obviousness, and the court fully considered the secondary considerations buttressing the conclusion that the invention of Boyd Schiltz was not obvious.

Although the Eighth Circuit had finally found a patent valid, *Woodstream Corp. v. Herter's Inc.*, in which I second chaired Bob Edell (which will be discussed later in detail), and although Judge Nichol had written a great opinion, affirmance by the Eighth Circuit was not a slam dunk. The Eighth Circuit's reputation was that it was a graveyard for patents. Until *Woodstream* in 1971, the Eighth Circuit from 1966 had held all sixteen patent cases before it invalid on obviousness.

Our opening comment in the brief for plaintiff-appellee before the Eighth Circuit states, "Lahman does not openly attack any significant finding of fact of the trial court as being clearly erroneous." In the argument section of our brief, we make the following strong statements: "Lahman's approach on appeal is to ignore the findings of fact. Lahman does not attack the findings of the court on the scope and content of the prior art, on the differences between the prior art and the claims at issue, on the level of ordinary skill in the art, on the fact that the invention was the first chain-type mover, and on the fact that the chain-type mover has numerous advantages over the prior art cable-type movers. Lahman does not attack the fact that there were problems with the prior art cable-type movers, that others had failed in trying to solve the problem, and that the invention was a contribution to this art. Rather, Lahman presents this court with a hodgepodge of patents and charts in the hope that the court will ignore the evidence and findings of fact to hold the patent either invalid or not infringed. That approach didn't work before the trial court (see PB supra p.7), and there is no evidentiary basis for it to be successful here. The findings of fact made by the trial court are fully supported, and there simply isn't a factual basis to support a conclusion other than that the Schiltz patent is valid and infringed."

The Eighth Circuit opinion is reported at 568 F2d 112 (8th Cir. 1978). In its opinion, the court stated, "It is not our function to try this case de novo. We are required to accept the factual findings of the district court unless clearly erroneous, Fed. R. Civ. P. 52(a), and if the district court applied correct standards of law to the acceptable facts of the case, its judgment must be affirmed.

"From our consideration of the record, we are satisfied that the factual findings of the district court are adequately supported by the evidence, and that the district court did not err in applying the law to the facts. Accordingly, we affirm the district court's judgment and do so principally on the basis of the opinion of Judge Nichol, which we consider to be detailed, painstaking, and well reasoned."

A great result. It is hard for me to believe that this Eighth Circuit opinion handed down January 11, 1978, occurred thirty years ago. I am advised from the Eighth Circuit opinion that Bob Edell and I were in trial eighteen days—not as long as either the National Connector case or the Lambert Industries case, but considering the time in Sioux Falls for some days before the trial started, it was at least three weeks. I might conclude by noting that Lahman petitioned the United States Supreme Court for a writ of certiorari, we briefed in opposition, and the petition was denied.

HURON V. CMI

This case is reported at 201 USPQ 111 (D. S.D. 1978). We represented the plaintiff, Huron Manufacturing Company. The suit was for declaratory judgment that the patent was invalid and not infringed. Our local counsel, who probably brought me the case, was good friend Deming Smith, a well-respected lawyer in Sioux Falls, South Dakota. In reading the decision, I was surprised to learn that Judge Nichol, who had decided the *Farmhand v. Lahman* case (discussed above) in September 1976, decided this case in our favor on July 28, 1978. The case is an interesting one, although I have little recollection of it except that the client and I went by Learjet to Oklahoma City to visit CMI's attorney, Jerry Dunlap. I've forgotten why we went to Oklahoma—perhaps a deposition or settlement meeting. But it was my first and only trip in a Learjet. It was a great flight. It must have been a one-day trip because I recall the pilot and plane waited for us at the airport, and we flew back that same day. The client probably flew from Sioux Falls and picked me up in Minneapolis.

Another thing that surprised me, in reading the decision, was that Mike Schwegman was on the case with me. I have no recollection of working with Mike on litigation. This must have been the only time.

We brought a motion for summary judgment on the basis that CMI should be collaterally estopped from asserting the validity of the patent in suit. What made this motion unusual was that the patent in suit had not been previously litigated. The collateral estoppel claim was premised on the holding in *CMI v. Lakeland Construction Company*, 184 USPQ 721 (1975), in which the claims of a related patent, the '026 patent, were held obvious in light of the prior art. Although the Lakeland case did not decide the patent in our suit, the '846 patent, to be invalid, the court in Lakeland held that the alleged inventions of the two patents were not patentably distinct. Our argument on summary judgment was that since the '026 patent and the '846 patent were not patentably distinct, they were equivalent. Thus, the same prior art applied to both patents, which rendered the '846 patent invalid.

It was CMI's position that the prior case applied only to certain claims of the '026 patent, that different claims were at issue in the '846 patent, and that the law of Blonder-Tongue, 402 U.S. 313 (1971) addressed only the relitigation of the same claims of a single patent.

Judge Nichol found that all of the factual inquiries were resolved in the '026 patent litigation, that no genuine issues of fact remained, and that CMI was to be collaterally estopped from asserting the validity of the '846 patent, the patent in our suit.

What a coincidence—I finished writing the above this morning before going to my regular exercise session at the Minneapolis Club. While returning to the office, I ran into Mike Schwegman in the skyway. So I stopped to chat about the case with Mike. He remembered working on the case shortly after joining M&G as an associate. He went with me on the Learjet ride to Oklahoma City and also recalled that as a highlight.

BERGSTROM V. SEARS

I don't personally have copies of the briefs filed in this case, but I have the reported decisions for reference. If my recollection is correct, this was Judge MacLaughlin's first patent case. Before starting the trial, he questioned counsel as to why this wasn't a jury case. I told him that we had a great case, and I wanted a good decision from the court, rather than from a jury, on the appeal of the case.

The invention of the plaintiff, Ted Bergstrom, our client, was in the design of a new fireplace grate. A copy of Figure 1 of Bergstrom's U.S. Design Patent U.S. No D-228,728 is reproduced below.

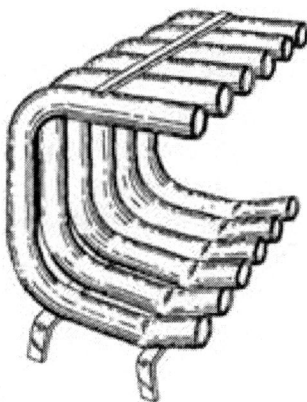

FIG. 1

Ted's patent was issued on October 23, 1973. The first trial against Sears and its supplier, Cardinal Foundry and Supply Co., was decided by Judge MacLaughlin on August 17, 1978. The decision is reported at 457 F. Supp. 213 (D.Mn. 1978). The sole issue at the trial was whether the patent was invalid because it was on sale and/or in public use more than one year before the filing date of the application for patent. Ted had prepared a fact sheet with photographs of his new fireplace grate, and five hundred copies were printed before the critical date of the filing of his application for patent. Also, a prototype grate was located in the recreational room in his basement. There, prior to the critical date, it was viewed by guests of his children and friends of the Bergstroms. Because of these events, the defendants argued the invention had been available to the public and on sale.

The court found that the five hundred fact sheets had not been used, except for one copy, which had been mailed to a Mr. Dryden of *Parade of Progress* to induce him to include a write-up of the fireplace grate in his column. Also, the disclosures of the fireplace grate prototype in Bergstrom's basement were incidental disclosures to casual adult visitors and to children who were present in his home for the purpose of visiting his children and not of viewing the fireplace grate.

Two notable events occurred at trial. Don Sell was our legal expert, and after he had finished his direct testimony, Judge MacLaughlin called counsel to the bench and said to me, "What do you think you are doing? You put this lawyer on the stand to tell me what the law is, and then to tell me what facts I should find to apply to that law. What do you think you are doing?" I apologized to the court for not making him aware prior to trial about the practice in patent cases to use a patent expert in this way. I also noted that it was particularly important for the court to observe the cross-examination of such experts. Chuck Steffey, attorney for the defendants, stepped in to help me because their only—or at least primary—witness was also a patent attorney legal expert. Judge MacLaughlin relented and said we could go forward with the case.

The second notable event was my cross-examination of the defendants' expert. James Gambrell Jr. was a noted patent lawyer from Texas. He taught courses in patent law, was a published author of numerous articles, and was a much-respected expert witness. The real controversy at trial was whether the fact sheet was accessible to the public. First, I had an article by Mr. Gambrell that contradicted his position at trial, and the nail in Mr. Gambrell's coffin was that he was unaware of the most recent decision by the Court of Customs and Patent Appeals on the law of printed publication. Gambrell could not wait to get out of the witness chair and, indeed, out of the courtroom. He was totally discredited, and Judge MacLaughlin found the patent not invalid under 35 U.S.C. 102(b).

On appeal, the defendants argued Judge MacLaughlin erred in his legal conclusions. The Eighth Circuit, in the appeal, which was argued by me and by Dennis Allegretti of Chicago, disagreed with the defendants and affirmed, per curiam, Judge MacLaughlin. This appeal is reported at 599 F.2d 62 (8th Cir. 1979). So the case went back to Judge MacLaughlin for trial on the issues of infringement, validity, and damages. The case was tried by me and Doug Williams for Ted Bergstrom and by Jon Nelson and Tim Malloy of the Allegretti firm of Chicago. I don't recall any notable events in this trial except that we were very successful and Judge MacLaughlin awarded the plaintiff a judgment against Cardinal, the manufacturer of the infringing grates, of $1,063,619.50, and a judgment against Sears of $391,575.00. This opinion is reported at 496 F. Supp. 476 (D. Mn. 1980).

The defendants appealed this decision to the Eighth Circuit. Sears and Cardinal retained new counsel to conduct the appeal, and Cardinal retained William Kraus of Cleveland, Ohio, to explore settlement. Kraus called me to arrange a meeting in Minneapolis to discuss settlement. That a settlement was reached is reported in Judge MacLaughlin's opinion reported at 532 F. Supp. 923 (D. Mn. 1982). From that decision come two facts of interest. Apparently, we retained Larry Brown and Steve Schroer of Faegre & Benson to represent Bergstrom because both Williams and I would be witnesses at trial on the settlement issue. On the settlement negotiations, I have no present recollection except I was interested to learn from Judge MacLaughlin's opinion that during an extended telephone conversation between myself, Doug Williams, and Mr. Kraus, I became upset and did not participate in the negotiations after that point. It's clear Doug Williams took the laboring oar in settling this case. He was probably helped by our partner, Cecil Schmidt, who was a good friend of Ted Bergstrom. What upset me and why I didn't further participate in the settlement of this case will remain a mystery unless one asks Doug Williams or Cecil Schmidt. As a part of the settlement, Ted Bergstrom assigned his patent to Cardinal, I assume to be able to treat the settlement sum as a capital gain. On April 15, 1982, Cardinal dedicated the entire patent to the public.

VEKAMAF HOLLAND V. PIPE BENDERS INC.

Doug Strawbridge helped me in the trial of this very interesting case for breach of a written secrecy agreement, patent infringement, and misappropriation of trade secrets. We represented the defendants, Marvin and Robert Meierhoff, father and son, of Duluth, Minnesota, and their company, Pipe Benders Inc. The product at issue was a huge pipe-bending machine built by the Meierhoffs and put in operation in Duluth.

The case was scheduled for trial before Judge Miles Lord, but the parties consented to trial before a magistrate, and the case was tried before Magistrate McNulty in Duluth. The trial started July 7, 1980, and ended July 25. As the appellate court noted in the first appeal of this case, 671 F.2d 1185 (8th Cir. 1982), the case included thirteen days of testimony, an inspection of the defendants' operations, extensive post-trial briefs, and a sixty-nine-page report of the magistrate, containing involved findings of fact and conclusions of law recommending dismissal of the patent infringement and misappropriation of trade secrets counts. See 211 USPQ 955 (D. Mn. 1981).

The plaintiffs filed 151 pages of detailed objections to the magistrate's recommendations. We had a hearing before Judge Miles Lord, and he adopted the magistrate's recommendations in toto and entered final judgment dismissing the complaint. The plaintiffs appealed to the Eighth Circuit. John Haley of Sidley & Austin argued for the plaintiffs, and I argued for the defendants. I recall the court brought to my attention a California decision and asked me to comment. I was unfamiliar with the case, so I must have bumbled through my argument. In any event, the Eighth Circuit remanded the case to Miles Lord to "analyze and discuss the plaintiffs' objections and the magistrate's report in order to provide proper and discernible grounds for appellate review." Miles Lord was given 120 days to certify his reasoned response to the plaintiffs' objections and his reasons for adopting the magistrate's report. See 671 F.2d 1185 (8th

Cir. 1982). The Eighth Circuit and Miles Lord were often at odds, and I was concerned Judge Lord would take offense at this remand. I was surprised by Judge Lord's opinion on remand. It was very thorough and detailed. I heard later that he had really gotten into this case and wrote his opinion himself.

So, we went back to the Eighth Circuit. Two additional lawyers from Sidley & Austin were added to the appeal, a Richard Flynn and a Richard Young. Since he was placed first, I assume Richard Flynn made the argument for the plaintiffs, and I, with Doug Strawbridge's good help, argued for the defendants.

Vekamaf initially contended that Miles Lord's opinion was not a reasoned response to its objections and thus failed to comply with the Eighth Circuit's order. The Eighth Circuit found the district court's order upon remand addressed Vekamaf's major objections seriatim and thoroughly discussed the pertinent findings made by the magistrate.

As the Eighth Circuit noted, "The foundation of Vekamaf's [patent] case rests on the premise that the bending of large diameter metal pipes can be accomplished by only one process, and that process requires the use of Vekamaf's patented link or equivalent sensing device for the control of lateral forces." One outrageous argument of the plaintiffs' was that the "defendants lacked the education, experience, or intelligence necessary to design and construct a pipe-bending machine with the capability of the defendants' machine." I've forgotten Bob Meierhoff's educational background, but he was very intelligent and capable, and he had made a detailed study of various pipe-bending machines.

We had a plant inspection of the Meierhoffs' pipe-bending machine, which included all the lawyers, the parties' experts, and Magistrate McNulty. The plaintiff's patented process had a floating pivot point or link, allowing the center point of the bending arc to move around. Bob Meierhoff insisted the defendants' machine didn't have that. Doug Strawbridge recalls the plaintiffs' lawyers suggested that Meierhoff must have taken it off of the machine specifically for the court's inspection. Doug recalls a conference in McNulty's chambers after a day of trial, when plaintiffs' top guy made that argument, and Bob Meierhoff called their bluff—he proposed that he would bend any size pipe that the plaintiffs brought to Duluth while the court watched (and would see that there was no floating pivot in the machine). If he could not successfully bend the pipe, he would concede the case, but if he could successfully bend the pipe and not break the machine, the plaintiffs would concede the case. The plaintiffs would not accept the challenge. As Doug says, McNulty never said anything about this exchange in his memorandum, but he always felt it was a turning point and a deciding factor in the case. Doug also recalls watching the bending process, which moved so slowly, it was sort of like watching ink dry.

John Strait was our expert witness, and he did his usual superb job. The plaintiffs' expert was a Dr. Caron. I recall him as being short, stocky, and very pompous. He strutted about the courtroom, trying to run everything for the plaintiffs. Judge McNulty found Dr. Caron to be a very learned man, but "his testimony was weakened by dogmatism, bias, and blatant advocacy of Plaintiffs' cause." Doug seems to recall that plaintiffs' attorney was a kind of disheveled, rather pompous guy from Sidley & Austin's DC office. This presents quite a contrast to the meek, unassuming manner of John Strait, Doug Strawbridge, and myself.

McNulty made an interesting comment on infringement. He said, "Initially, the court was somewhat confused, if not mislead, by Plaintiffs' dwelling at length upon an argument directed towards establishing that the defendants have not proven that they have not infringed the patent in suit." On appeal, the Eighth Circuit found there was substantial evidence in the record to support the magistrate's recommendation and the district court's conclusion that Vekamaf failed to prove patent infringement by a preponderance of the evidence.

On the misappropriation of trade secrets, plaintiffs had some twelve trade secrets alleged to have been used by the defendants. The plaintiffs' twelfth trade secret, which they called a compendium, was a total of all the individual trade secrets. The magistrate found that most of the alleged trade secrets were not trade secrets at all within the meaning of the law and that others had not been improperly acquired or used by the defendants. The Eighth Circuit affirmed, 696 F.2d 608 (8th Cir. 1982).

Although the Circuit Court was referring to the issue of the credibility of witnesses, its comment is of interest: "Our review of the record does reveal a morass of confusing, conflicting, and sometimes incredible testimony, but it does not leave us with the 'definite and firm conviction that a mistake has been committed.'" I think the court was referring to the plaintiffs' testimony. We put on a great case with some daunting adverse facts relating to the Meierhoffs' visit to

Vekamaf to view their process; together with the implication the Meierhoffs intended to purchase a Vekamaf machine; but instead of buying a Vekamaf machine, the Meierhoffs built their own machine. The Meierhoffs were great clients, and I believe they really appreciated the job Doug Strawbridge and I did on this very interesting case.

MEDTRONIC INC. V. CPI

I have a clear recollection of most of the cases I have tried. It is curious that I have no war stories of this case and no clear recollection of either the trial or the appeal. Perhaps I have erased this case from memory because the case was lost at the district court and on appeal. Perhaps it's because the CAFC so severely criticized me for my comments in the appeal brief about Judge Devitt. Unfortunately, I have not been able to find copies of our briefs in this case, and several boxes in storage have been transferred out. All I have are the courts' decisions and some time records for part of 1981.

This case, entitled *Medtronic Inc. and Med-Rel Inc. v. Cardiac Pacemakers Inc.*, is reported at 555 F.Supp.1214 (D. Mn. 1983), affirmed, 721 F.2d 1563 (CAFC 1983).

The case involved three patents: Greatbatch patent, U.S. 3,391,697; Wingrove patent, U.S. 3,833,005; and Walmsley patent, U.S. 3,901,247. Doug Strawbridge helped me in the trial and appeal of this case. Also, I note from my time sheets that Al Underhill had some involvement early in the case. I have time sheet records only until August 21, 1981, when we went to computer billing.

From observing the time records I have for 1981, I had a very busy schedule. I was working on three Medtronic cases: *Medtronics v. Intermedics, Vitatron v. Medtronics,* and this case. The Intermedics case was venued in Texas, and our local counsel, Tom Arnold's firm, took over the case. The Vitatron case was settled.

July 9, 1968   W. GREATBATCH   3,391,697
RUNAWAY INHIBITED PACEMAKER

Filed Sept. 20, 1965   3 Sheets-Sheet 1

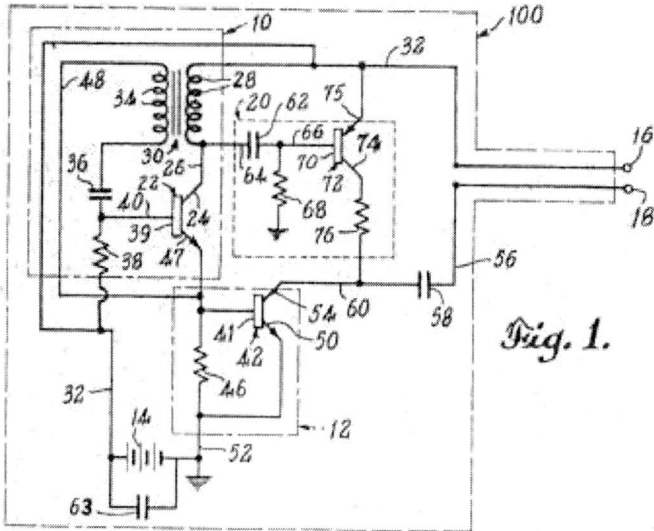

Fig. 1.

Judge Devitt found each of the patents novel, but obvious over the prior art. He did not decide the infringement issues. We, I know, put on a great case. In hindsight, this should have been a jury case, and the result would have been more favorable. But at this point in time, jury trials were uncommon in patent cases, and I was more comfortable trying a case to the court.

Looking at my time records for 1981, I worked a lot of Saturdays and Sundays. In March 1981, I had a trial in *Farmhand Inc. v. Anel Engineering* in Lubbock, Texas; June 29-July 1, I was in Buffalo, New York, for the deposition of Wilson Greatbatch; July 6 and 7, I was in Moline, Illinois, on the Deere v. Farmhand case; July 8, I flew to LA for depositions in this case and was in depositions July 9 and 10; I left LA on the 10th for a hearing in Lubbock, Texas, in the *Farmhand v. Anel* case on the 11th; and I returned to LA for depositions July 13–16.

During this time period, I was working on a number of cases: *3M v. Eco-Chem,* the Pipe Benders case, *Litton v. Whirlpool, Farmhand v. Lahman,* the Wilkening case, *OMC- Keller v. Clark,* and *3M v. Rynne.*

The district court trial of *Medtronic Inc. v. CPI* took place for seven days commencing September 7, 1982. Judge Devitt's decision is dated January 19, 1983. The appeal decision by the CAFC is dated November 23, 1983. The attorney for CPI was Tim Malloy of the Allegretti firm in Chicago.

I wish I had my time records for 1982. They might help me understand why I have so little recollection of this case. I know I went to El Paso, Texas, May 19 and 20, 1981, on a personal matter, which may have involved my son Jim.

On to the next case.

SCHERING CORP. V. PRECISION-COSMET CO.

This was a patent infringement case in which we represented the defendant. This was my first jury trial. Doug Williams second chaired me at trial. I believe the case took place in Wilmington, Delaware. I do not have any briefs, and the case was not reported. I do recall some events at trial. Precision-Cosmet had its own patent. The trial court refused to let me introduce any evidence on this patent on the grounds that it would confuse the jury; and its potential prejudice out-weighed any relevance. Since the plaintiff's infringement case rested on the doctrine of equivalents, I maintained it was very relevant to show a substantial difference between the patented product and defendant's product. I also recall plaintiff's evidence of infringement was not to read the claims on defendant's product; but rather, to show only the similarity of plaintiff's commercial product and defendant's product. Of course, the jury assumed the plaintiff's product was the patented product; and since our product was similar to plaintiff's product, defendant must infringe. This evidence was introduced over my strong objections. I also recall that the judge gave me a very hard time in laying the foundation for one of our exhibits. It was a minor matter; but it did embarrass me in front of the jury. So, the jury found for the plaintiff. I thought we had a good appeal. The client obtained other counsel who took over the case; and the case was settled by a license pending the appeal.

FARMHAND AND REYNOLDS V. ANEL ENGINEERING IND.

Mentioned in connection with the *Medtronic v. CPI* case, this case was tried in March of 1981. It involved Farmhand's patent on its chain-type haystack mover. Reynolds was a licensee of Farmhand, making truck-mounted chain movers for loading and moving large stacks of cotton rather than hay. This also was a jury case, which took place in cotton country, Lubbock, Texas. Doug Strawbridge second chaired me in this case. I've forgotten the issue, but in arguing our position before the court, Doug had found a great case supporting our position. The judge complimented Doug on finding a "strawberry" case. That must be a Southern expression, and it must mean a case right on point. One particular event at trial involved the prior favorable decisions by the Eighth Circuit in *Farmhand v. Craven* and *Farmhand v. Lahman*. On a motion in limine, I was not permitted to refer to these decisions. However, the defendant's own expert, on direct examination, referred to the prior decisions. I immediately moved the court to introduce the decisions into evidence, which was granted.

This case was particularly interesting because one element of the claim called for "hay"-engaging teeth. The defendant's movers were not engaging hay, but cotton.

As an aside, I engaged the very well-known Texas patent lawyer, Tom Arnold of Arnold, White, to be my expert. For those who might know Tom well, you know he didn't use simple words. He was always very eloquent, but with a very large, and sometimes complicated, vocabulary. I worked with Tom to get him to express himself very simply so the jury would understand. We also had on board a Lubbock, Texas, general practice lawyer, Warlick Carr, to take some of our witnesses so the jury didn't perceive us to be Northern carpetbaggers.

The trial went very well, and the jury found in our favor. The defendant appealed. The appeal decision by the Fifth Circuit is reported at 693 F.2d 1140 (5th Cir. 1982). I was surprised to be reminded when reading the decision that it was written by Circuit Judge Politz, because Circuit Judge Brown was very active during oral argument. Judge Brown was a very humorous judge, and I wish I could remember his specific quips during argument. I like Judge Politz's statement:

"This case involves a truly intriguing device, which reconfirms the accuracy of the adage that necessity is the mother of invention. The device at issue is commonly called a chain-type, or chain-beam, haystack mover. The haystacks involved are not the wigwam-shaped piles brought to mind by references to Little Boy Blue or to searching-for-a-needle-in, but are large, tightly packed bales measuring fifteen by twenty-four feet and weighing up to ten tons. The chain-type mover has been adapted to handle the cotton module, a recently developed cotton bale similar to the haystack but heavier."

3M V. ECO-CHEM

Stephanie Rynne, her parents, and sister owned Conversion Chemical Co. Her husband, George Rynne, was an employee of Conversion. In 1974, 3M bought Conversion and acquired its patents. After the sale, George Rynne worked for 3M as general sales manager in the acquired business. George Rynne left 3M in February 1977. The next month, George and Stephanie established Eco-Chem Inc., a Minnesota corporation. In 1978, prior to this suit, the Rynnes left Minnesota and moved to Georgia.

In January 1979, 3M commenced this action for infringement of the patents acquired from Conversion. After seven extensions of time, Eco-Chem (ECI) answered, admitting jurisdiction and venue. 3M served ECI with interrogatories and request for documents. In the interim, the Rynnes decided to disband ECI. ECI's response to the discovery requests was as follows:

"Defendant, Eco-Chem Inc., is an inactive Minnesota corporation with no employees and with no operations in Minnesota or elsewhere. Consequently, Defendant is unable to respond to Plaintiff's first set of interrogatories and first request for production of documents."

On 3M's motion, and after hearing (at which ECI was represented by counsel), District Court Judge Harry MacLaughlin entered a default judgment of patent infringement and entered an injunction.

In late 1979, the Rynnes established Eco-Chem Ltd. (ECL), a Georgia corporation. The stockholders of ECI exchanged their stock for ECL shares. The Rynnes converted all of the assets of ECI to ECL. They informed their customers that ECL had succeeded ECI. ECI became judgment proof.

On August 15, 1980, 3M moved in the Minnesota District Court to add the Rynnes and ECL as parties. All parties were served. After a hearing on the motion, at which the Rynnes were present, the district court granted the motion to add the Rynnes and ECL as successors in interest and alter egos of ECI. The court ordered post-judgment discovery and a hearing on an award of damages.

Although the record doesn't reflect this, I believe that the Rynnes failed to respond to 3M's post-judgment discovery. We brought a motion to hold the Rynnes in contempt of the court's orders. Judge MacLaughlin found George Rynne in contempt and ordered him jailed until he complied. This order was transmitted to the federal marshals in Georgia, and George Rynne was jailed just before Christmas, 1983. He remained in jail until after Christmas. We joked that when questioned by cellmates, Rynne would say he was found guilty under 35 USC 281.

By order of March 16, 1984, the court awarded 3M damages, attorney's fees, and prejudgment interest. The total award was $751,508.59.

On April 3, 1984, the defendants filed a motion for a new trial or for modification of the default judgment. This was denied, and the defendants appealed to the Federal Circuit. I argued the appeal at the CAFC.

On March 15, 1985, the CAFC affirmed the district court's decisions denying the defendants' motions for relief from the judgment and for a new trial.

After this decision, I believe 3M reached a settlement with the Rynnes on the outstanding judgment. I was not involved in the settlement.

This was a very interesting case involving a default judgment against a judgment proof Minnesota corporation (ECI); getting the responsible parties, the Rynnes, added as parties; a holding of George Rynne in contempt and putting him in jail over Christmas; and ultimately, a successful CAFC opinion. This is the only case of patent infringement that I know of in which a party spent time in jail.

DR. JERRE FREEMAN V. 3M

This was a suit for infringement of U.S. Reissue Patent 31,640. The patent involved Dr. Freeman's invention in intraocular lenses. Walt Kirn, one of 3M's patent lawyers, was in charge of the case. He had done all of the discovery in the case. Walt asked me to second chair him in the trial of the case in Wilmington, Delaware. To be second chair is a piece of cake. No problem, I readily agreed. However, the problem arose when a month before trial, Walt said, "John, I want you to try this case. I'll second chair you."

But back to the beginning. Freeman filed suit against 3M October 5, 1984. Freeman also filed suit against CooperVision, and the two cases were consolidated for trial, except damages, if any, were to be the subject of separate trials. There were two preliminary motions decided by the court, in which I am identified as being of counsel for 3M. I recall being present at some hearings before Judge Caleb Wright, and I must confess, I was not initially impressed with his capabilities. Walt Kirn must have handled the heavy lifting at these hearings.

One, reported at 661 F. Supp. 886 (D. Del. 1987), was a motion brought by Freeman to enjoin 3M from seeking reexamination of the patent in suit. The motion was denied, with the court deciding it would continue to hear the case. The second matter involved motions for summary judgment filed by CooperVision and 3M. The motions for summary judgment were denied, reported at 675 F. Supp. 877 (D. Del. 1987). 3M's motion primarily sought a claim interpretation, pre-Markman hearings, to require a lens with an overall mean density substantially the same as the aqueous humor. This interpretation would exclude "sinking" IOLs, which described 3Ms lenses. The judge decided that the dispute over claim interpretation could not be resolved by examination of the prosecution history alone. The court decided it needed expert testimony to resolve the meaning of disputed terms.

United States Patent [19]

Freeman

[11] E   Patent Number: Re. 31,640

[45] Reissued Date of Patent: Aug. 7, 1984

[54] [NEUTRAL] BUOYANCY INTRAOCULAR LENS DEVICE

[76] Inventor: Jerre M. Freeman, Ste. 503, Crew Wing, 176 S. Bellevue, Memphis, Tenn. 38104

[21] Appl. No.: 44,032

[22] Filed: May 31, 1979

Related U.S. Patent Documents

Reissue of:

[64] Patent No.: 4,077,071
Issued: Mar. 7, 1978
Appl. No.: 666,681
Filed: Mar. 15, 1976

[51] Int. Cl.² A61F 1/16; A61F 1/24
[52] U.S. Cl. 3/13
[58] Field of Search 3/13, 1; 351/160

[56] **References Cited**

U.S. PATENT DOCUMENTS

2,834,023	5/1958	Lieb	3/13
3,711,870	1/1973	Deitrick	3/13
3,906,551	9/1975	Otter	3/13
3,925,825	12/1973	Richards et al.	3/13
3,975,780	9/1976	Boniuk	3/13
4,010,496	3/1977	Neefe	3/13

OTHER PUBLICATIONS

"Artiphakia and Aniseikonia" by R. C. Troutman,
American Journal of Ophthalmology, vol. 56, No. 2, Oct. 1963, pp. 630-639.

"A Weightless Iseikonic Intraocular Lens" by Richard O. Binkhorst et al, American Journal of Ophthalmology, vol. 58, No. 1, Jul. 1964, pp. 73-78.

"The Weightless Intraocular Lens" by R. C. Troutman, Ophthalmic Surgery, vol. 8, No. 3, Jun. 1977, pp. 153-155, 3-13.

Primary Examiner—Ronald L. Fricke
Attorney, Agent, or Firm—Bradford E. Kile

[57]   **ABSTRACT**

A neutral buoyancy intraocular lens device, adapted for implantation in a human eye and having an optical lens portion and support members attached thereto for holding the lens in place, is provided with a portion having a mean density lower than the density of the aqueous humor of the eye and a size large enough to decrease the mean density of the entire device to substantially the same as the aqueous humor of the eye to produce neutral buoyancy relative thereto, thereby increasing the compatibility of the device with the human user's eye and reducing trauma to the eye. The low-density portion may be an integral part of the lens and support structure, or may be a separate member attached thereto, and the lower mean density may be achieved by the use of a void or a relatively low density material.

22 Claims, 6 Drawing Figures

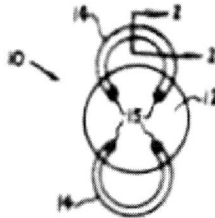

Just before trial, CooperVision settled with Freeman, and this left 3M as the only defendant. As mentioned, Walt Kirn had done all of the discovery, which was quite voluminous, including depositions in Russia of the director of the Moscow Eye Institute. I left Walt to be in charge of our technical experts, and I recall getting Don Banner and Don Chisum as our patent experts. Chisum was a professor of law in Seattle and the well-known author of the treatise *Chisum on Patents*. I recall traveling to Seattle, before we had an office there, to prepare Don Chisum to testify.

This trial took place March 1–15 and April 4, 1988. The weather must have been nice in Wilmington because I recall walking with Don Chisum in a park, working on his testimony. The only other clear recollection I have of this trial is that Carl Moy, a Japanese-American associate with M&G, taught me to like sushi. Carl left M&G and is a well-respected professor of patent law at William Mitchell Law School in St. Paul.

Judge Wright handed down his decision on August 29, 1988, reported at 693 F.Supp. 134 (D. Del. 1988). Intraocular lenses (IOL) are implanted into the eye to replace a natural lens. Dr. Freeman's invention basically involved increasing the buoyancy of the lens in the eye by altering the composition of the support for the lens, the haptic, without altering the optical portion of the lens.

Judge Wright's infringement analysis followed the two-step process of first construing the language of the claims, and then applying the properly construed claims to 3M's IOLs in suit.

There were several claim terms in dispute. I will refer to just two key terms. First, Claim 1 specified that the buoyancy means "reduce the overall mean density of the lens device to substantially that of the aqueous humor." Freeman testified that this condition was met when there was any reduction in density caused by using buoyant supports. It was 3M's position that the claim required "neutral buoyancy."

The judge gave a well-reasoned opinion finding Freeman's definition to be incorrect and holding that the limitation required reducing the density of the lens to close to neutral buoyancy, thus creating a condition wherein the lens would weigh near zero in aqueous humor. A second key finding related to the phrase "at least a degree of buoyant uplift." Judge Wright noted that most of the trial involved interpreting this phrase and attempting to distinguish it from the language of Claim 1, referred to above. Freeman again argued that this phrase meant reducing the density and weight of the device by any amount, even if the reduction was not to a state of neutral. 3M argued that an object with buoyant uplift must possess neutral or positive buoyancy.

The court found the specification did not aid in defining the term, and although the prosecution history shed some light, it did not reveal a clear definition.

Judge Wright found he had to consider expert testimony. Freeman's expert was an MIT mechanical engineering professor, and 3M's was from the University of Minnesota. In addition to referring to the parties' technical experts, the court noted that 3M's legal expert, Donald Chisum, had opined that 3M's interpretation was correct because it gave meaning and substance to the claim.

The court held 3M's interpretation to be correct and that "buoyant uplift" required at least neutral buoyancy. Since all of 3M's lenses in suit, some sixteen styles, would sink in aqueous humor, the court found no infringement.

In addition, the court gave a detailed discussion of the prior art and his opinion that all of the claims in suit were invalid. I will not discuss this in detail because on appeal, the Federal Circuit decided there was no occasion to review the judgment of invalidity in view of its affirmance of the court's findings of no infringement.

On appeal, reported at 884 F.2d 1398 (Fed. Cir. 1989), the Federal Circuit noted that the district court, in rejecting Freeman's interpretation of the claims (particularly the phrase "degree of buoyant uplift"), had relied upon the specification, the prosecution history of both the original patent and the reissue, and the expert testimony. Based upon all of this evidence, including the testimony of 3M's experts (which the court credited), the court concluded that the claims were limited to implants that were at least neutrally buoyant in aqueous humor.

The appellate court found that the district court's conclusion, above noted, was not erroneous and that its finding of no infringement, based upon its interpretation of the claims, was not clearly erroneous.

In spite of these adverse decisions, Dr. Freeman did not give up. You will recall that at the beginning of reporting on this case, I had referred to Dr. Freeman moving the court to enjoin 3M from filing for reexamination of his patent. The court denied that motion, and in anticipation that 3M might seek to stay the litigation pending the reexamination in the patent office, the court held that it would continue to hear the case in spite of 3M proceeding in the patent office with reexamination. The court said, "With or without the PTO's assistance, the court will be able to rule on the issue that could be decided by the PTO reexamination process."

The importance of the court's ruling in this respect is made evident when we refer to what happened in PTO proceedings. Before doing so, however, I will note that Dr. Freeman filed for rehearing en banc, which was denied September 30, 1989, reported at 1989 U.S. App. Lexis 14958, and he petitioned the United States Supreme Court for a writ of certiorari, which was denied April 2, 1990, 494 U.S. 1070 (1990).

The case of Re Freeman is reported at 30 F.3d 1459 (Fed. Cir. 1994). The reexamination of Freeman's Reissue Patent 31,640, filed by 3M on May 8, 1987, was granted by the PTO; however, the PTO, *sua sponte*, suspended the reexamination upon commencement of the trial before Judge Wright. The PTO examiner finally rejected Freeman's reissue claims as impermissibly seeking to enlarge the scope of the claims as interpreted by the district court. Freeman appealed the examiner's rejection to the Board of Patent Appeals and Interferences. The board affirmed the examiner; however, the board did not agree with the interpretation of the reissue claims by the district court. The board stated, in no uncertain terms, that "the district court's finding and holding with respect to the limitation 'at least a degree of buoyant uplift'... is totally contrary to what the appellant (Dr. Freeman) always intended the limitations to denote."

In spite of its disagreement with the District Court, the board felt constrained to accept the court's interpretation of the claim language and affirmed the examiner. Dr. Freeman appealed to the Federal Circuit. On appeal, the Federal Circuit applied the doctrine of issue preclusion or collateral estoppel. The court concluded, "Because Dr. Freeman had a full and fair opportunity to litigate the identical issue of the meaning of the term 'buoyant uplift,' an issue actually decided in the district court and essential to the finding of noninfringement in that action, application of issue preclusion is appropriate here." Further, the court found no circumstances precluding application of the doctrine.

So, after some ten years of litigation, Dr. Freeman found that his interpretation of his claim language was correct, but Judge Wright's decision in the 3M case precluded that interpretation. All I can say is that we put on a great case at trial in support of our claim interpretation and negating Freeman's interpretation. The district court had much more evidence before it on the meaning of the disputed claim terms than the PTO had. Thank goodness the PTO's interpretation by the Board of Patent Appeals did not precede our trial.

CASES WHERE I ASSISTED AT TRIAL

DAVID MANUFACTURING COMPANY ET AL. V. SPECIALIZED PRODUCTS INC. ET AL.

Robert Edell was lead counsel in this case, and I second chaired him. I believe this was Bob's first trial as lead counsel. Our client, David Mfg. Co., was exclusive licensee of U.S. Patent 3,156,541 on an apparatus for drying grain, in particular corn.

Prior to Henry Kalke's invention, there were two common methods used in drying corn. In the batch drying method, a small amount of corn, about one foot in depth, was placed on a perforated floor. The corn was dried quickly by high-temperature air introduced through the perforated floor. After drying, the corn was unloaded from the bin, and a new batch of corn was put in. This method required a lot of work, loading and unloading the bin and closely monitoring the air temperature to ensure the corn was not overdried. The second method was called stage or layer drying. In this method, a first layer was placed on the perforated floor of the drying bin to a depth of three to four feet; this layer was dried and left in the bin. A second layer was placed on top of the first layer, and after drying, a third layer was placed in the bin. In this method, it was necessary to hold the moisture content of the drying air at approximately 55 percent relative humidity with 70 degrees ambient air temperature. The disadvantage of this method, although less work than the batch method, was that it was very slow. It could take several weeks to dry one bin full of corn.

Kalke's invention was to combine a stirring mechanism with the drying bin. The stirring mechanism comprised a mounting arm movable in an orbital path above the corn in the bin and a stirring auger extending into the bin, which was movable radially in and out with respect to the orbital path of movement of the mounting arm.

This invention revolutionized in-bin grain drying. It combined the best features of both batch and layer drying; it allowed the farmer to use the high temperatures of the batch drying in a full bin of corn as used in the layer method.

I recall two main events occurring at this trial. The defendants' expert was a Dr. Fisher, dean of electrical engineering at, I believe, the University of St. Louis. On direct examination by the defendants' counsel, Dr. Fisher made what I believed was a gross error in his statement of the law. He hadn't really hurt us in his direct testimony, and I believed we could destroy him on cross.

By the time Dr. Fisher finished his direct testimony, the day was over, and Bob and I retired to our war room to prepare a devastating cross. As we studied the law issue, Bob became convinced that Fisher was laying a trap for us. He hadn't made a mistake, and he was saving his best testimony for cross. So Bob started his cross the next morning by announcing that we had no questions for Dr. Fisher. He left the stand, leaving his best potential testimony unsaid. I was very impressed by Dr. Fisher, and I used him later in some cases that I tried.

A second event that I recall was that after both parties had rested, the court congratulated both counsel on their fine presentations; he just had a couple of questions. First, he wondered what the "prior rot" was that the parties had referred to, and second, he discussed the German prior art reference in terms that were very damaging and showed a misunderstanding of that reference. In view of the court's questions, Bob immediately moved to reopen our case to recall our expert, Prof. John Strait, to answer the court's questions. It was a good and successful move. The judge's decision in the plaintiff's favor is reported at 324 F.Supp.588 (S.D. Ill. 1970).

WOODSTREAM CORPORATION V. HERTER'S INC. AND GEORGE L. HERTER

This was a landmark case in the Eighth Circuit. Bob Edell was lead counsel, and I second chaired him. The District Court case was tried before Chief Judge Edward Devitt. His decision, dated May 7, 1970, is reported at 312 F. Supp. 369 (D. Mn. 1970). Two patents were involved, U.S. 3,010,245 and 2,947,107. Both related to animal traps.

Aug. 2, 1960   J. U. LEHN   2,947,107

ANIMAL TRAPS

Filed Sept. 18, 1958

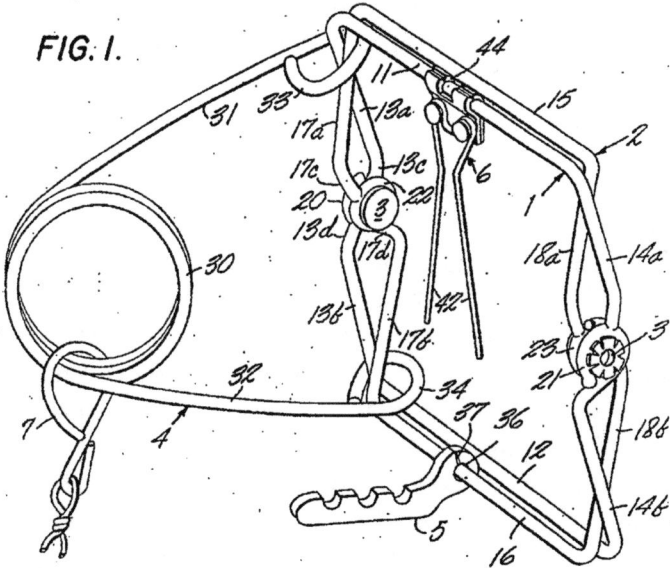

FIG. I.

Judge Devitt noted that the courtrooms within the province of the Eighth Circuit Court of Appeals did not afford a congenial forum to the holder of a United States patent. He found the patented animal traps to be a substantial improvement over the long-spring, coil-spring, and jump traps which had long been in use by trappers.

After citing all of the features and advantages of the patented trap, Judge Devitt held:

"Notwithstanding the greater utility, humaneness, and commercial success of the Conibear type trap, factors certainly entitled to consideration when determining patentability, it appears to the court that the features which characterize the Conibear and Lehn traps over the prior art are such as would be obvious to a mechanic skilled in the trap art at the time of the patenting of the Conibear and Lehn traps." He found the patents invalid as obvious.

Judge Devitt also denied the plaintiff's claim for unfair competition.

We had some wonderful witnesses at trial. Mr. Elihu Abbott was a professional trapper from New Jersey. He was a champion muskrat skinner who had won many prizes. He came from a long line of trappers and made his living trapping muskrats. He was a character. I doubted he had ever stayed in a hotel before this trial. He was not well educated, but he was not awed by testifying before a federal judge. He displayed great poise and confidence, scaring us by setting various traps in the courtroom and demonstrating how they worked. After a day of trial, we would go back to the hotel to our war room, and Eli would regale us with stories of burying government revenue agents in the swamps of New Jersey. He made a wonderful witness.

In addition to Eli, Bob introduced considerable evidence showing that Mr. Conibear, as a result of his new trap, had received the only award ever given by the American Humane Association (AHA) for the development of a humane animal trap. Another important witness was Arthur Harding, publisher and editor of Fur-Fish-Game magazine for over forty years. He testified about the terrific impact of the Conibear trap on the trapping industry.

On appeal, the Eighth Circuit finally held a patent valid. The court reversed Judge Devitt's finding of invalidity with regard to the Conibear patent and remanded the case for further proceedings on the issue of infringement. The court wrote a very thorough opinion reported at 446 F. 2d 1143 (8th Cir. 1971). I will not repeat the details of this opinion except to note the court's comments on the defendant's expert.

"On the instant appeal, the plaintiff-appellant focuses his primary attack upon the crucial testimony, which led the district court to reject the Conibear patent. The defendants' expert witness, admittedly possessing no experience in the trap art, could not state which elements should be taken from the Mau patents and which elements should be taken from the Ullman patent to 'construct' this anticipatory combination. [As an aside, Bob did a superb job of cross-examination.] In light of the other testimony and evidence introduced, we think Appellants' objection to the district court's reliance upon the defendants' expert witness is well taken."

In summary, the court held that the record here demonstrates that the defendants failed to sustain their burden of proof; accordingly, the validity of the Conibear patent must be sustained. A great decision and a great victory. This case catapulted Bob Edell into national recognition.

ENDERES TOOL CO. INC. V. ORIGINAL ENDERES COMPANY

Our client was the Enderes Tool Company. This was a trademark case brought against the Original Enderes Company for using the mark "Enderes" on tools and in their name. I recall very little about the case except that I went alone to Guttenberg, Iowa, to take depositions of the defendant. For some reason, I asked Alan Carlson to take the lead in this case. Doug Strawbridge, an associate in the firm, was assisting and keeping track of our numerous exhibits. I asked Doug for some of his recollections of the trial, and he forwarded to me pages 627 and 628 of the transcript. Dave Bothum of Enderes Tool Company was on the stand, identifying exhibits showing confusion. Alan Carlson was questioning the witness. First, he referred Dave Bothum to the plaintiff's exhibits 369 and 369A. These numbers reflect the large number of exhibits at trial.

When Alan referred to the next exhibit, 370, Judge Donald Alsop interrupted and stated, "I think that's a duplicate, Mr. Carlson, with 352." Mr. Carlson acknowledged that it is a duplicate.

Ken Siegfried, the attorney for the defendant, stated, "Could we find the document marked 352? Because this appears to be the original."

The Court: Then the other one was, perhaps, a copy.

You're in big trouble, Mr. Strawbridge.

Doug had the judge sign page 628 of the transcript, and it stated:

> Dear Doug,
> My best wishes for a successful legal
> career.
> Signed, Judge Don Alsop
> January 9, 1976

My notes indicate this case was won by the plaintiff after a partial trial in January 1976. It must have been settled after over six hundred pages of testimony by the plaintiff. We had overwhelming evidence of confusion.

NORTHWEST BANK AND TRUST V. NORWEST CORP.

I have very little recollection of this case except that Doug Williams was lead counsel for Norwest Corp., and I was second chair. This was a suit for trademark infringement tried in Des Moines, Iowa. My notes indicate that it was a win for our client, the defendant, Norwest Corp. This case at the time of my notes was not yet reported, pending a request for reconsideration by the plaintiff. I have asked Doug Williams for information about the trial, and his only war story relates to the incident of Doug either cross-examining the plaintiff's expert or examining our witness in such excruciating detail and repetition that everyone, including the judge, was bored to death. Apparently, I grabbed Doug by his coattails and whispered, "Enough is enough."

I wish I could recall more about this trial. In any event, it turned out to be a major victory for Doug Williams.

MEDTRONIC INC. V. DAIG CORPORATION

I don't have much to report on this case because I was not very heavily involved. I was initially when the suit was filed. I was also initially involved with the *Medtronic v. Intermedics* case filed in the U.S. District Court for the Southern District of Texas. I obtained Tom Arnold's firm in Houston, Texas, as local counsel, and they ended up taking over the case. Bob Edell was primary counsel, and he was aided by Al Underhill of our firm and by Joe Breimeyer, in-house counsel for Medtronic.

The case started in May 1979. In August 1981, Pacesetter Systems Inc. filed a D.J. action against Medtronic in California. This case was transferred to Minnesota and consolidated with the Daig case. There was considerable pretrial maneuvering as outlined by Judge Earl Larson in his opinion reported at 611 F.Supp. 1498, 227 USPQ 509 (D. Minn. 1985). This case was a great victory for Bob. The case focused on Claim 1 of Medtronic's U.S. Patent 3,902,501 (the '501 patent). The invention related to an endocardial electrode or lead having a plurality of pliant nonconducting tines adjacent the electrode tip to better fix the lead in the heart. In a lengthy and well-reasoned opinion, Judge Larson found the '501 patent valid and infringed by a number of Daig's leads and a number of Pacesetter's leads. The trial took place February 14, 1985, to March 20, 1985. Judge Larson rendered his decision on June 24, 1985.

On appeal, the CAFC, 789 F.2d 903 (Fed. Circ. 1986), affirmed Judge Larson.

JACKSON A. SMITH, INDIVIDUALLY AND DBA RAND PATENTS INC. V. CONDUX CORPORATION

This was a suit in state court in Mankato, Minnesota. Smith sued Condux for breach of contract and for misappropriation of trade secrets.

In the first instance, Condux was represented by patent attorney Dick Bartz. Smith won a favorable summary judgment. Condux then contacted M&G, and the matter was directed to Jack Clifford, who got me involved. We recommended getting Bob Sheran of Lindquist & Vennum as lead counsel with me to handle the patent issues. Mr. Sheran was a former justice of the Minnesota Supreme Court. L&V successfully overturned the summary judgment against Condux with a Rule 60 motion. This permitted Condux to assert a number of defenses: breach of contract by Smith; Smith induced Condux to enter into its license agreement by fraud and misrepresentation; the licensed patents were invalid and not infringed; there was inequitable conduct during the prosecution of the application for patent; there was patent misuse; and Condux further counterclaimed that Smith had committed unfair competition.

By way of background, Smith owned four U.S. and four Canadian patents relating to cable pulling eyes. The U.S. patents were 3,989,400 for a pulling eye; 4,070,894 for a crimping device; 4,337,923 for a fiber optical cable pulling eye; and 4,411,409 for a lubrication system. Before coming to Condux, Smith had granted an exclusive license to Chip-N-Saw, a division of Hawker Siddeley Group Ltd. A disagreement arose between Smith and Chip-N-Saw, which was settled. Smith contended the license with Chip-N-Saw was terminated, and he offered a nonexclusive license to Condux. Smith's license to Condux in January 1982 had a favored nations clause, which, provided that if Rand Patents, Smith's company, entered into a settlement agreement or a paid-up license with another licensee, Smith's license gave Condux the right to adjust its royalty rate. Condux requested Smith to provide information relating to its settlement with Chip-N-Saw. When the information was not forthcoming, Condux placed its royalty payments into a bank account. Smith advised Condux the license was in default for failure to pay royalties. Smith then initiated this lawsuit.

This was an eleven-week trial before a jury. The trial transcript is over eight thousand pages. Fortunately, my role dealt with the patent issues, and I did not have to be and was not at the trial all eleven weeks. Most of the trial time was taken up by Smith. The trial judge was Harvey Holtan, an extremely patient and capable judge. There were interminable conferences in chambers. The differences between Smith's lead counsel, Jack Dominick, and Condux's lead counsel, Bob Sheran, was striking. Bob Sheran was tall, calm, soft-spoken, and always a gentleman, and Jack Dominick was rotund, bombastic, and argumentative.

Condux prevailed at trial on all points. The evidence demonstrated that Smith as a licensor under the license agreement with Condux neither existed nor owned the patents. Further, Smith breached the favored nations clause and tried to coerce Condux into buying the patents. Thus, the jury could have reasonably found a justification for Condux withholding royalty payments and that Smith's actions prior to any withholding by Condux was a breach of the agreement by Smith.

The jury also found patent misuse and that the funds in the bank belonged to Condux based on the misuse. In addition, the jury found no patent infringement and that Smith had engaged in unfair competition.

Of great importance is the fact that the trial court awarded Condux costs and attorney fees in the amount of $1,006,595.60, which was affirmed on appeal. See *Smith v. Condux,* Court of Appeals of Minnesota, 1990 Minn. App. Lexis 943.

Smith had a Canadian company called Copperthorne that was in competition with Condux. Smith and Copperthorne were advertising that Condux was an infringer and had no right to sell pulling eyes.

Post-trial, the court granted an injunction against Smith and, for violation of that order, granted extraordinary relief in a temporary restraining order. See *Smith v. Condux,* 466 N.W. 2d 22 (Mn. Ct. of Appeals 1991).

Smith fortunately was financed by a Mr. David Duack, and a confirmed letter of credit with the Toronto Canadian Bank secured the more than $1,000,000 award. I'm not sure what all Jack Clifford did, but he was given the task of going to Toronto to collect the money.

Jack recalled an incident at trial where I was cross-examining a witness for Smith on the patent issues; Bob Sheran left the counsel table to sit in the back of the courtroom. As the cross-examination progressed, Bob Sheran kept moving up toward the front until he was in the front row, fully engrossed in my cross-examination. He later commented, Jack recalled, "Watching John Gould examine a witness is like watching Bjorn Borg hit tennis balls."

I thoroughly enjoyed working with Bob Sheran and Dave Allgeyer of Lindquist & Vennum on this case. Jack Clifford and Paul Lacy were in Mankato for all eleven weeks of trial and were of tremendous support to me and to the L&V trial team. This case was a first in having patent issues of validity, infringement, and misuse at trial in a Minnesota state court.

A NUMBER OF CASES SETTLED BEFORE TRIAL

I was involved in a number of cases that settled before trial. I don't have much detail about them. I will merely cite what is in my log of cases:

Montana-Dakota Utilities, A Trademark Interference on the mark "Genie" (Interference No. 5402?) Won.

George Amonson v. Leef Bros. This was a contract matter in which we represented the defendant. Suit dismissed on nominal settlement.

Fingerhut v. Parker et al., an unfair competition suit in which we represented the defendant. Suit dismissed on nominal settlement.

Two suits: *Cleary v. A. R. Wood* and *A. R. Wood v. Lundeen.* The cases were settled.

Waco Mfg. Co. v. Washington Aluminum Co. Inc. A Cancellation of Registration No. 6920 and No. 6921. Case settled.

Sun Drop Sales Corp. of America v. Sun-Rise Inc. A cancellation of Registration No. 6907. I represented the defendant. Won a favorable dismissal by agreement and stipulation.

Waco v. Patent Scaffolding, a patent infringement suit for Plaintiff, Waco, dismissal with prejudice by stipulation.

Super Valu v. Quality Markets Inc., Civ. Act. # 58 C. 46, a trademark suit. Settled—obtained a favorable consent decree.

A. R. Wood & A. R. Wood Mfg. Co. v. Thompson et al. d/b/a F & F Supply and Produce. Case settled.

Matthews v. Cold Spring Granite Co. We were associate counsel. Nominal work on our part, favorable settlement reached.

Up-Right Inc. v. Aluminum Safety Products Inc. Lost a motion to dismiss for lack of jurisdiction.

Bastian-Blessing v. Vincent Brass & Aluminum Co., a patent infringement case. Settled with a consent decree of validity and infringement.

Niagara Therapy Mfg. Co. et al. v. Niagara Minnesota Company et al. Case settled.

A. R. Wood v. National Ideal Co., a patent case settled with a consent decree of validity and infringement.

Kermit H. Wilson v. Haldeman-Homme, a patent infringement case settled with a consent decree of validity and infringement.

Mayo Clinic v. Mayo Bros. This was a trademark case in which we represented the Mayo Clinic. The suit related to the defendant's use of "Mayo" on a mayonnaise product. The case was in the Minnesota District Court in Rochester. There should be a reported decision. Case won for the Mayo Clinic.

Rollei of America Inc. et al. v. Honeywell Inc. This case involved camera flash attachments. My notes only indicate that the case was settled. We represented Rollei of America and its German parent. Some things I recall about the case are that:

I flew into Frankfort, Germany, and was picked up by a driver to drive to Braunschweig, where Rollei Werke had its headquarters. I arrived a little before noon, exhausted, ready to go to my hotel and collapse. The chairman of Rollei Werke was pleased to learn that I was a Rotarian as he was about to leave for his Rotary meeting. I was his guest at the meeting, at which the language was German. Ready to go to my hotel after this meeting, I was taken back to the plant for an afternoon of work.

I remember a deposition of the chairman in the United States, either in Minneapolis or in Chicago, where Honeywell's attorneys were located; Dennis Allegretti was lead. The chairman wanted to testify in German, and the first problem was with Honeywell's translator. Rollei's U.S. counsel, whose name I have forgotten at the moment, spoke German like a native. He recognized the translator's problems. We finally resolved this issue by having Rollei's U.S. counsel act as the translator. A deposition with translators is very tedious. The question is asked in English, it is translated into German for the witness, and the witness replies in German, which is then translated into English. I'm not sure what Allegretti had implied, but all of a sudden, my witness stood up, pointed his finger at Allegretti, and said, in English, "I am the chairman of Rollei Werke, and I am telling you the truth."

Another event I recall was going to MIT and investigating their thesis files for early publications of a man named Edgerton, a pioneer in the art of flash photography. We must have found some good prior art because the case was shortly settled.

Kayo Oil Co. v. Kunz Oil Company. I represented the Kunz Oil Company in this trademark dispute. The Kunz Oil Company was owned by my good friend Walt Kunz. My notes only indicate the case was settled; however, I recall the Kunz Oil Company received a very substantial payment in settlement which was much appreciated by the client.

Carpenter-Taylor Company v. MCM Industries. My notes only indicate this was a contract matter which was settled. Carpenter-Taylor was a company owned by my friends and ex–fraternity brothers, Walt Carpenter and Steve Taylor. I believe this matter involved their patented invention in a water supply pressure tank having a floating disc separating the air and water. It helped prevent the loss of air in the tank, thereby maintaining an appropriate head of pressure for longer periods of time. I assume the matter was favorably settled for Walt Carpenter and Steve Taylor. Steve Taylor went on to invent a new sailboat, which we patented for him. The boat was called *Skylark* and was licensed to the Starcraft boat company, which produced the sailboat for several years. Steve arranged to have Starcraft give me a sailboat, which I had at Lake Vermilion many years.

Vitatron v. Medtronic Inc. We represented Medtronic, and my notes only indicate that it was a suit for patent infringement, which was settled.

Medtronic Inc. v. Pacesetter Systems. My notes only indicate that this was a suit for patent infringement settled "favorably" for Medtronic during trial. This case was venued in Miami, Florida. I don't recall much about the trial except that it occurred shortly after I had given up drinking any alcohol in an effort to encourage a son to stop drinking. After a day of trial, it was normal practice for me to go back to the war room for a couple of scotch and sodas before settling in to a night of preparation for the next day of trial. The war room was a separate hotel room set up with tables and chairs for all participants at the trial to gather and work. I recall riding the hotel elevator, after the first day of trial, up to the war room and having the taste of scotch in my mouth in anticipation of the drink I was not going to have. As an aside, my quitting all alcohol was not successful at this time as far as my son was concerned, but I have not had a drink since. My son later successfully went through treatment and has been sober many years.

I had another Medtronic case, which my notes indicate was settled. The case was *Medtronic Inc. v. Telectronics/Cordis.*

Multi-Arc Vacuum Systems Inc. v. Vac-Tec Systems Inc. This was a suit for patent infringement in which I represented the plaintiff. My notes indicate the suit was favorably settled for Multi-Arc at the time of trial. Both parties had filed numerous motions in limine. These are motions to exclude evidence.One motion I recall dealt with the fact that the invention was licensed by Multi-Arc from Russian inventors. At a pretrial hearing before Federal Judge Harry MacLaughlin, he commented that in all his years as a judge, he had never seen so many motions in limine. I wanted to remind the judge that most of his experience, before becoming a federal judge, had been as a judge of the Minnesota Supreme Court, where they wouldn't have any motions in limine. But I held my tongue. In any event, whether it was all those pending motions to decide or the complexity of the case, Judge MacLaughlin put a lot of pressure on the parties to settle. This worked to our advantage, and apparently, a favorable settlement was reached. I don't recall the details.

Skyline Displays Inc. v. Nomadic Structures Inc. I'm not sure how this case came to me because our client, Nomadic Structures, was in Springfield, Virgina. This was a suit for patent infringement in which we represented the defendant. My notes indicate that the suit was favorably settled before trial. Mark Schuman, who is no longer with the firm, aided me on this matter. I recall Mark went on to do further work for the client while he was at M&G, patenting their own innovative structures.

Nu Aire Inc. v. Mallinckrodt Inc. This case was a suit for patent infringement in which we represented the plaintiff. I recall Nu Aire was owned by Max Peters, and I had done work for him on several matters. My notes indicate the suit was favorably settled before trial. I have no recollection of this case, and I have had no contact with Nu Aire or Max Peters for many years. I wonder if they are still a client.

Flow Boy Mfg. v. Road Machinery & Supplies Inc. This case was a suit for patent infringement in which we represented the defendant. As I recall, the suit involved a large truck or tractor-pulled trailer for asphalt with a side delivery feature. I don't recall much about this case. My notes indicate that it was favorably settled before trial.

Lull Engineering v. Selleck Equipment et al. I have no recollection of this case. My notes indicate it was a suit for patent infringement in which we represented the defendant. My notes also indicate the suit was favorably settled.

3M v. Dacar Inc. I have no recollection of this 3M case. My notes indicate that it was suit for patent infringement in which I represented plaintiff, 3M. The suit was concluded with a consent decree of validity and infringement.

3M v. Pfizer. This was a suit filed by our client, 3M, for declaratory judgment of invalidity and no infringement. I have no recollection of the case. My notes merely indicate it was settled. I assume it was favorably settled for 3M.

Weldon Farm Products Inc. v. Walden Farms.

I'm not sure this is the Weldon Farm Products case in which I assisted my partner Cecil Schmidt; however, the case I am familiar with was venued in California. There were several defendants.. Cecil and I went to Los Angeles for depositions of the defendant located there. We had served the defendant with a very broad document request. At the deposition, it became clear that the defendant had not produced all of the documents requested. They had not objected to the document request. While Cecil continued with the deposition, I worked on a motion to require production of all documents requested. Working with our local counsel, we obtained an emergency hearing on the motion that very afternoon. I recall that when we appeared before the judge, he told the witness, pointing to a front-row seat, "You sit there and stay there until I hear this motion."

The judge was pretty upset with the defendant and ordered the company to produce all documents requested by the next morning. A van arrived the next morning at the situs of the depositions with boxes and boxes of documents. The volume was such that it was clear the defendant's counsel had not reviewed the documents being produced. When Cecil and I began to review the newly produced documents, we found several that could have been withheld as privileged. These documents were devastating for the defendant and resulted in a quick and favorable settlement.

When Cecil and I went to depose the second defendant in San Francisco, we had a very different result. There, the defendant had moved to quash our request for documents as being too broad and overreaching. The judge decided in the defendant's favor, and we didn't get the same scope of documents as in Los Angeles. Cecil continued as lead counsel on this matter. I don't recall the result, but it must have been favorable because Henry Weldon continued to be a friend and client.

As an aside, I should tell a story about Henry Weldon. He had a gorgeous, large apartment near Central Park. It was decorated, at the time I visited, with antique paneling from England.

Henry was redoing his apartment and asked his architect to be on the lookout for some suitable paneling for a room of his apartment. The architect found some, but it required Henry to purchase the contents of a barn in upstate New York. Just before the paneling was to be delivered, Henry arranged for a small basement room or closet to store the paneling until needed. The van arrived, and Henry took the driver downstairs to show him where to put the paneling. The driver took Henry outside to the van and said, "Look, bud—there is no way this is going to fit in that closet." It was a huge van, filled to the brim with stuff. The contents of the barn were not just paneling for one room. It included enough to panel Henry's whole apartment—marble bathroom fixtures with gold faucets, etc., etc. It turned out to be just a huge treasure trove.

Susan Maxwell v. J. Baker

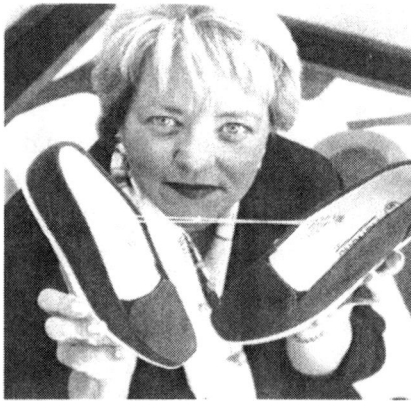

The firm yesterday put on a CLE for two credits of bias. The CLE involved lectures by Sue Maxwell concerning gender bias she had encountered in her profession and in the litigation involving her patent; by Diane Wiley, a jury consultant; and by Dan McDonald, one of our trial lawyers who was involved in Sue Maxwell's litigation.

Sue Maxwell was a buyer in the shoe department of Target Stores. While in this position, she conceived an invention for connecting mated pairs of shoes to prevent mismatching when offered for sale in self- service stores like Target. She had two male associates in her department, and she disclosed her invention to them. One of the men went to Target's counsel to disclose the invention and claim it as his own. Target's counsel thought the invention might be patentable and arranged for their outside counsel to prepare a patent application. Sue found out about this and immediately told Target's counsel that the invention was hers. He advised her to get her own patent attorney. She had a friend who had a brother for whom I had apparently done some work, and I was recommended to Sue. She came to me with the problem and reported back to Target's counsel that I would be getting in touch with him. Sue reported back to me that his response was, "I told you to get a patent attorney, not to get the best."

I worked out an arrangement with Target that Sue Maxwell would own the patent on her invention and that Target would have a shop right to use the invention, provided it marked their product with her patent number. This helped Susan in her later marketing of her invention and in recovering damages.

Sue discovered substantial infringement of her patent by the industry. All users, other than Target, circled the wagons and refused to license her patent. Sue was forced to sue for patent infringement, and our firm took the cases on a contingency agreement.

The first defendant was J. Baker Company, and the case went to trial before a jury with Judge David Doty presiding. I thought my involvement had ended with working out the agreement with Target that Sue would own the patent on her invention, but Sue reminded me yesterday that I helped in some of the depositions, and while our trial counsel were preparing for the second trial on damages, I had appeared on her behalf at a settlement conference.

After years of depositions and trials, Sue ultimately prevailed in her suits against the industry. I don't know the full extent of her compensation, but it was several million dollars. My partner, Earl Reiland, was lead trial counsel, aided by Dan McDonald, who I believe was lead in some of the later trials.

The list of cases goes on and on; for many cases, I have little information, except that they were settled. Creative *Arts v. Helen's Rainbow Paints* (copyright infringement), *La Maur Inc. v. Bo Dean Beauty Supply Inc. et al.* (patent infringement), *Burn-Zol v. Atlas Incinerator Co.* (patent infringement, *Dole Valve v. Sperzel Co., The Kelling Nut Co. v. Johnson Nut Co. et al., Jerrold Stephans Co. v. the Whirley Corp., Warning Lites Inc. v. Saf-T Flare of Minn.,* etc., etc.

I will refer to one case of interest. *Technograph Printed Circuits Ltd. v. Bureau of Engraving Inc.,* Civil Action No. 63–86 JWC N.D. Cal., Central Division. Technograph had allegedly invented the printed circuit board. I represented the Bureau of Engraving in this suit for patent infringement.

There were many defendants all over the country. We were just one of several defendants in California. I was at a pretrial before the court. A criminal matter was on for hearing before our cases. The defendant appeared to make a preliminary plea, and the judge banged his gavel down and announced that he found the defendant guilty on all counts. The judge's clerk ran up and whispered in the judge's ear, and the judge apologized that he was thinking of another matter and withdrew his guilty pronouncement.

And this was our judge. He began blocking out his calendar for months, setting specific trial dates for the defendants, each case to follow upon conclusion of the case before it. Most of the defendants in court with my case had government contracts, and their civil liability was minimal, so they were settling with Technograph. I began to think I might be the only one left for trial. Fortunately, the judge, whose guilty finding earlier may have been a precursor, had a stroke and was taken off my case. This delayed the trial enough so that an earlier case, I believe in Maryland, came to trial with an adverse finding for Technograph. Technograph was a British company; if they had prevailed, the damages would have paid Britain's war debt. A memo was found in which the inventor was reporting back to his British lawyers. From memory, the memo said: "Well, we certainly put something over on the U.S. patent examiners at our interview today. They thought they were allowing very narrow claims, but in fact, we have been allowed very broad claims." As a result of this memo, the court found Technograph had misled the patent office and found this basic printed circuit patent to be invalid. As a result of this decision, affirmed on appeal, we were able to successfully move to dismiss the case against the Bureau of Engraving on the grounds of res judicata.

At the conclusion of my notes setting forth the results of thirty-two cases, twenty-six tried by me and six at which I assisted, there is the following statistical information:

Of the thirty-two cases that went to trial, twenty-seven were patent infringement cases, four were trademark and unfair competition cases, and one involved both patent and trademark issues.

Of the twenty-eight patent cases, fourteen were for alleged infringers and fourteen were for the patentee. Thirteen of the alleged infringer cases were won; one was lost but then settled. Ten of the fourteen patentee cases were won; four were lost. Three of the patent cases were jury trials. The plaintiff jury case was won; one defendant jury case was won, and one defendant jury case was lost.

All four trademark cases were won.

SOME CONCLUSIONS

I was lead counsel for 3M in a very big case involving their competitor, the Norton Company.

The Norton Company has its headquarters in Worcester, Massachusetts. I was flying to Boston, renting a car, and driving to Worchester with boxes of documents for a week of depositions. This occurred several times in the discovery phase of the case. Fortunately, I was home when I had my heart attack. I was in the habit, when home, of driving to and walking around Bredeson Park in Edina in the morning. I did so the day of my heart attack, but found when I got there that I had no energy to take my usual walk. Not aware of any problem, I just went home and dressed to go to the office. At some point in the morning, I walked up the stairs from my office floor to the firm's library. Upon doing so, I broke into a sweat and just didn't feel good. So I decided to go home. We had our house at 5600 Interlachen Circle up for sale, and I was supposed to pick up a dining room light fixture that was in for repair. Again, I had no energy to do so. As I was lying on the living room couch, probably late afternoon, I began having severe pain down my left arm. My wife was on the phone, and as I rolled on the floor in pain, I tried to signal her to call for help. She was on the phone with my sister, who can be difficult to cut short in conversation. To make a long story short, Mary called the doctor and drove me to Abbott Northwestern's emergency room, where I was immediately given a wonder drug to prevent clotting. An angiogram showed my main descending artery to be almost 100 percent plugged. The doctors immediately proceeded with angioplasty to ream out the plugged artery. This was pre-stent; however, the procedure was very successful.

This heart attack forced an end to my litigation career. Doug Strawbridge, a partner of the firm, had been aiding me in the Norton case, and 3M approved him taking over the lead in the case. Up to this point in time, 3M had been a major client for me and the firm. Doug Strawbridge fitted well with 3M's culture, and they were pleased to have him continue to fill my role. Doug, working with 3M's in-house patent attorney, Dick Francis, successfully worked out a major settlement with the Norton Company.

I may have mentioned that I was contacted by a person in our document retention department to determine the fate of several boxes with my name on them. I had them delivered to my office to review. In my office, I still have two of the boxes, filled with old briefs, speeches I have given, some correspondence, etc. I will mention only one document of interest. I was asked by general counsel for the Atlas Incinerator Company to aid them in responding to the plaintiff's motion to strike the action from the jury calendar. I found this to be a very interesting project. I wish I still had the brief I wrote because it turned out to be a challenging issue. I did a lot of research even into British Common Law and wrote a very good brief. The matter came on for hearing before U.S. District Judge Edward Devitt in April 1962. The judge, in his decision dated April 10, 1962, said:

The law is far from clear; in fact, it is confusing and contradictory, as to whether a jury trial is available as a matter of right in a patent case.

The court has considered the well-prepared briefs of counsel on each side, and concludes that Defendant is entitled to a jury trial; that Plaintiff's motion that the case be stricken from the jury calendar is denied.

My notes on this case only indicate that it was settled. Probably Judge Devitt's decision was a big factor in bringing the plaintiff to agree to settle the case.

Hindsight is a wonderful thing. I guess I failed to appreciate, in 1962, the importance of trying a plaintiff's patent case to a jury. I certainly wish I had tried *Medtronic v. CPI*, discussed above, to a jury. It took some twenty years before it became common practice to try patent cases to a jury. I was asked by Judge MacLaughlin at the start of *Bergstrom v. Sears,* also discussed above, why the case wasn't being tried to a jury. I responded, "Judge, I have an excellent case in which the plaintiff will prevail, and I want a well-written opinion by the court, which will be affirmed on appeal."

If I dig hard enough, I may find a few other cases decided on summary judgment without a trial, but it's time to bring this history to a close. But before I do so, I should mention two important trademark matters involving rather famous marks. I was retained by Honeywell to help them register their round thermostat as a trademark. Honeywell had design patents on their round thermostat that had expired. To continue protection, Honeywell had filed for trademark protection. Their applications were rejected on the grounds that the design, upon expiration of their patents, was in the public domain and not protectable as a trademark. I haven't found any briefs or files, so relying on memory, I believe this rejection was appealed to the Trademark Trial and Appeal Board, where I convinced the board that the round thermostat was indeed a famous mark which could coexist with patent protection and was registrable.

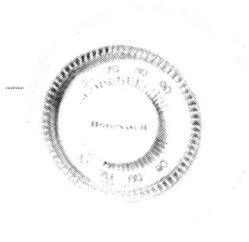

The second interesting trademark matter was the registration of the mark "Softsoap" for a detergent. This application was rejected by the Patent and Trademark Office as being merely descriptive of a soft soap, citing various dictionaries and old recipes for making soft soap. I sued the Commissioner of Patents in Minnesota to require registration. We put together a vast amount of evidence showing a difference between soap and detergent and that in fact the term "Softsoap" was publically recognized as a trademark of Minnetonka Company. Counsel from Washington, DC, representing the Commissioner of Patents, reviewed our evidence and gave up the fight. "Softsoap" was registered and has become very well-known as a mark for liquid hand soap.

Softsoap ®

After reading through the final draft of this book before going to press, I realized my notes on cases tried were incomplete. I'd left out the important case of Litton Systems, Inc v. Whirlpool Corp, 728 F.2d 1423 (Fed. Cir. 1984). I can't find a cite to the wonderful decision by Judge Magnuson, District of Mn., in Litton's favor on all points. Unfortunately, the Federal Circuit reversed. Another case of interest, in which I did all of the pre-trial discovery, was a case for the British

Post Office which Alan Carlson tried in Colorado. Perhaps there are others; but too late to add into this book that is long enough as it is.

I have been fortunate, and I have had a wonderful career as a lawyer. When I started with Ralph Merchant some fifty-six years ago, I was the second lawyer. Now we have over one hundred lawyers with offices in Seattle; Denver; Omaha; Madison, Wisconsin; Atlanta; Knoxville, Tennessee; Washington, DC; New York; and of course Minneapolis. Since my heart attack, my main job has been writing opinions for clients. This involves giving product clearance on a client's new or improved product and providing opinions on whether a client's patent is being infringed by a third party or whether a client might infringe a third party's patent. How long I will continue coming into the office almost daily is not yet known. As long as my health is good and the firm doesn't kick me out, I still enjoy the mental rigor of my chosen profession.